MW00861492

Helmut Jahn
Werner Sobek
Matthias Schuler

Architecture Engineering

WERNER BLASER

HELMUT JAHN
ARCHITECTURE
ENGINEERING

HELMUT JAHN
WERNER SOBEK
MATTHIAS SCHULER

Birkhäuser – Publishers for Architecture
Basel · Boston · Berlin

Translation of Werner Blaser's essay from German into English:
Elizabeth Schwaiger, Toronto

A CIP catalogue record for this book is available from the Library of
Congress, Washington D.C., USA.

Deutsche Bibliothek Cataloging-in-Publication Data

Helmut Jahn, Werner Sobek, Matthias Schuler - architecture engineering /
Werner Blaser. - Basel ; Boston ; Berlin : Birkhäuser, 2002
ISBN 3-7643-6734-2

© 2002 Birkhäuser – Publishers for Architecture, P.O. Box 133, CH-4010
Basel, Switzerland.
Member of the BertelsmannSpringer Publishing Group
Printed on acid-free paper produced from chlorine-free pulp. TCF ∞

Layout: Werner Blaser and Keith H. Palmer

Litho and typography: Photolitho Sturm AG, Muttenz

Printed in Germany

ISBN 3-7643-6734-2

9 8 7 6 5 4 3 2 1   http://www.birkhauser.ch

CONTENTS

The architect Helmut Jahn from Chicago and the engineer Werner Sobek from Stuttgart have been instrumental in advancing the integration of architecture and engineering. Their material technological developments in steel and glass make a façade system possible which is independent of load-bearing framework components and regulates light and heat. The technological foundations on whose basis the architect and engineer develop the construction lead to more complex, aesthetically sophisticated solutions: glass, the "liberating" building material of the 21st century, belongs to the pioneers and "puzzle freaks" whose experiments and inventions initiate self-supporting glass structures of great lightness and transparency. The roots of these building methods, and the technical-mathematical approach they follow, lie in current technologies.

Helmut Jahn has cleverly linked his projects to a techno-trend and created a useful tension in the structural and creative domain with his team of young engineers and technologists. We see the emergence of a total architecture, which has a profound impact on the urban context. The team adroitly promotes a balance between research and realization, terminology and design. Upon closer inspection, the technological-creative assumes a causal role in their most recent projects. Thus, in 1999, they developed a unique attitude through the trend-setting concept of "Archi-Neering": engineer and architect join in a partnership to form a design team.

The current shift in attitude towards technology, which is changing and influencing our time like never before, ideally illustrates the co-operation between the disciplines of architecture and engineering. The technological awareness is the medium for a new confirmation of identity, which reveals all human senses in the unity of the "ingenious" art. In the hands of Helmut Jahn, Werner Sobek and Matthias Schuler, contemporary architecture is the place where three disciplines come together, and where, above all, the possibility of a new building technology is under discussion. Without unnecessary splendour, developed in symbiotic collaboration, we see the gradual emergence of a world architecture that welcomes economical building and a matching lifestyle as a challenge. The credo of the much-praised and newly interpreted engineer-architecture is transparency, openness and internal flexibility. The load-bearing grid, exposed on the outside, creates light, weightless internal spaces – a flexible concept executed with analytical precision. Genius is born from finding the simplest solutions, finding form as a means of forming the self.

These details demonstrate that the innovative team lead by Helmut Jahn, Werner Sobek and Matthias Schuler has successfully built an information bridge for our time by integrating form, structure and technology. Their urban implants promise a quantum leap towards a new image of the city. The confidence, which a large project of technological monumentality promises, answers not only to a need for security, but also speaks of an understanding of contemporary urbanity as a cultural challenge. In the interest of dematerialization, a structural flow of form or serial revival, the uniqueness and exclusivity of a building is visualized in this instance as a team play between the architectonic form and the structure. Architecture has always been an art that translates visions into form. It is part of a realistically founded partnership of architect and engineer to tackle the new with passion.

Werner Blaser

HELMUT JAHN, FAIA

BIOGRAPHY

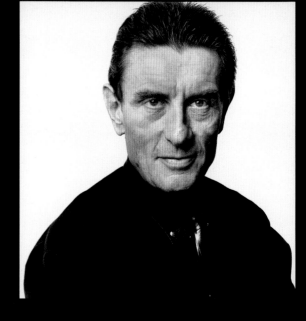

1940	Born January 4, 1940 in Nürnberg, Germany
1965	Graduated from Technische Hochschule, Munich, Germany
1965–1966	Worked with P.C. von Seidlein, Munich, Germany
1966–1967	Graduate studies at Illinois Institute of Technology, with Myron Goldsmith and Fazlur
1967–1973	Assistant to Gene Summers, C.F. Murphy Associates
1970	Married – Deborah Lampe from Chicago
1973	Executive Vice President and Director of Planning and Design, C.F. Murphy Associates
1975	Registered Architect NCARB; state registrations Illinois, California, Colorado, Connecticut, Florida, Georgia, Indiana, Minnesota, New York, New Jersey, Pennsylvania, Ohio, Texas, Virginia and Iowa, and Member of German Chamber of Architects, State of Hessen
1977	Selected for Inclusion in 40th Edition "Who's Who in America"
1978	Birth of son, Evan
1979	Owens-Corning Fiberglas Energy Conservation Award – Argonne Program Support Facility
1980	Honorary Degree Doctor of Fine Arts – St. Mary's College, Notre Dame, Indiana
1980	Selection for Inclusion in 5th Edition "Who's Who in Technology Today"
1981	Principal, Murphy/Jahn
1981	University of Illinois Circle Campus, Chicago Illinois, Visiting Professor at Design Studio
1981	Harvard University, Elliot Noyes Professor of Architectural Design
1982	President, Murphy/Jahn
1983	President and CEO, Murphy/Jahn
1983	Yale University, Davenport Visiting Professor of Architectural Design
1987	Fellow American Institute of Architects, in which his work has received seven American Institute of Architects National Awards and a total of 44 Distinguished Building Awards from local chapters.
1988	R.S. Reynolds Memorial Award for Distinguished Architecture Using Aluminum – United Airlines Terminal
1989–1994	Illinois Institute of Technology, Thesis Professor
1991	Ten Most Influential Living American Architects – American Institute of Architects
1993	Outstanding Achievement/Architect Award from the Illinois Academy of Fine Arts
1994	"Bundesverdienstkreuz Erster Klasse" of the Federal Republic of Germany
1998	The DuPont Benedictus Award
1999	The International Prize for Textile Architecture
2001	Urban Land Institute (Sony Center and HA•LO)
2001	National Design Building Award
2002	Imperial Bank Tower Renovation
	I.D.E.A.S. Awards for Innovative Design and Excellence in Architecture using Structural Design

Architecture/Engineering
Helmut Jahn/Werner Sobek/Matthias Schuler

In our practice we have been interested since the early 90's in the integration of technology and design. This has led over the last eight years to a most rewarding collaboration with Werner Sobek and Matthias Schuler with the goal of designing buildings in a totally integrated approach, breaking down the barriers which often exist between Architecture and Engineering.

When we worked in 1993 on the office buildings for Principal Financial Group in Des Moines and the Reedy Creek Improvement District in Orlando, we discovered that both the engineering profession and the construction industry had, in the aftermath of postmodernism and a developer servant industry, lost its desire and ability to do an architecture informed by principles of engineering and technology. The engineers lacked the vision and concepts and industry and suppliers favored more conventional construction and materials.

At that time our practice had also turned more global with projects in South Africa, Asia and Europe, with the majority in Germany. On those projects we could experiment more, the clients were often more challenging and daring. Minimum energy and the use of natural resources was an important goal. Engineers and the building industry were also committed more towards exploring the New.

In 1994, I became aware of the work of Werner Sobek and I met him briefly in Chicago, to where he had brought the students from his Institute in Stuttgart. This became the beginning of our extraordinary collaboration and friendship. Shortly afterwards we started to work together on the New Bangkok International Airport (NBIA), the Charlemagne Building in Brussels and the Sony Center in Berlin. NBIA, which is under construction now, required in its integrated approach not only

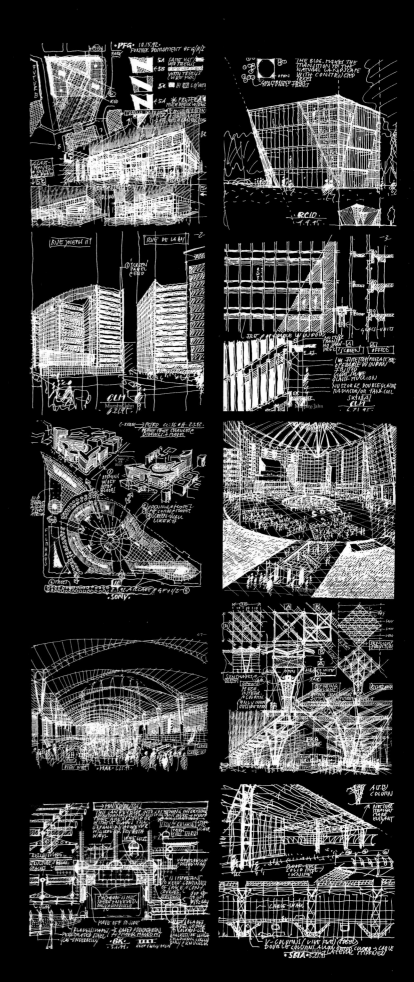

support in the area of structure and enclosure, but also for environmental and comfort-engineering. Together we interviewed several candidates in this field and selected Matthias Schuler, who co-founded Transsolar in Stuttgart. As a physicist he approached environmental engineering informed by science, use of minimal equipment, maximizing natural resources and increasing the comfort in buildings.

Today, as long as circumstances allow, we do all buildings together. We are thinking alike, aware of the others' discipline and in the course of discussion and exploration cross over into the others' fields. Architect and Engineer speak the same language. We have coined the phrase "Archi-Neering" to describe this working relationship. This starts often with finding a concept for a building together and carries through the design and workings of a buildings' structure, energy/comfort-systems and enclosure. Systems and components are not looked upon as separate, but integral building parts. For instance, the enclosure, which includes both façade and roof, is considered a component, which modulates the climate of a building and deals with daylight, natural ventilation, solar energy and their interaction with the buildings' technical systems. In the process the team works with specialists in the fields of glass, fabrics, plastics, coatings, aerodynamics and components, which heat and cool buildings and are often integrated with structure, façade, floor or ceiling.

This process leads to a further dematerializing and transparency of buildings. It is our belief that perfection can only be achieved when nothing can be taken away. It will be only a question of time when the façades of buildings become switchable barriers, which control light, view, sound and temperatures as needed. Façades and roofs act as fabrics which modulate the natural and the artificial light. They become screens, transparent, opaque, reflective or refractive. Light becomes the essence of the design. The buildings are luminous, not illuminated.

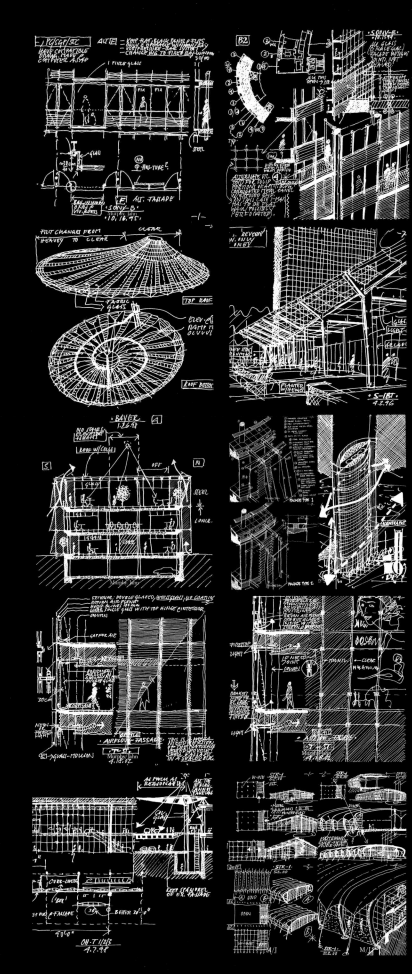

The work in this book shows the continued development and refinement of those ideas on façades and roofs, starting from Sony Center and the Neues Kranzler Eck to Bayer, Deutsche Post and Galeria Kaufhof to the Hochhausensemble am Münchner Tor, the Skyline Tower in Munich and the MAX in Frankfurt.

As much as Werner Sobek, Matthias Schuler and myself are concerned about the solution to technical problems in architecture, we constantly are aware and weigh the aesthetic and formal results of this work. The point is, that the architect thinks more about the technical consequences of the forms he designs and the engineers have to consider the aesthetic results of their concepts and decisions. Only such an approach leads to the integration of Architecture and Engineering.

Our collective work is characterized by a forward-looking attitude, a search for the "New", the "Cutting Edge", the "Boundaries". The "New" cannot become a purpose in itself and has to improve the environment and the surroundings in which we live. We are convinced that the human mind is greatly influenced by its architectural environment. The forms and the aesthetic of these structures affect everything from urban place making to the individual functions they house. The goal is to use the integration of architecture and engineering to improve the built environment and become representational of the 21st Century.

Helmut Jahn
September 2002

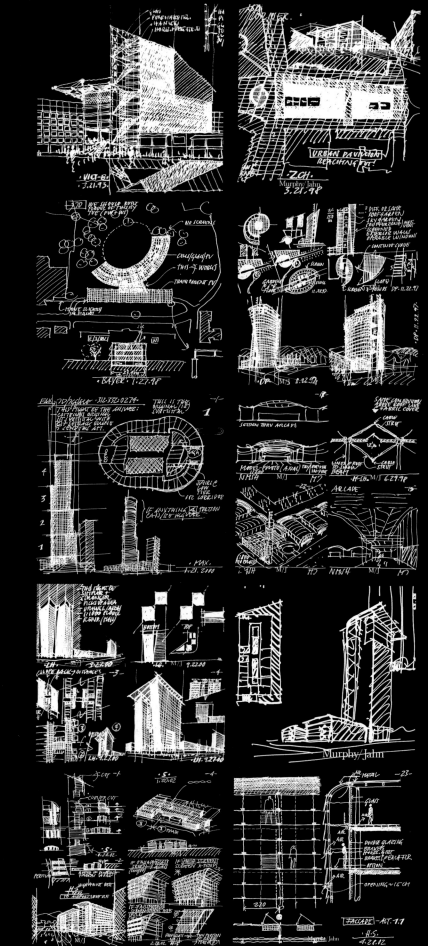

WERNER SOBEK

BIOGRAPHY

1953	Born in Aalen, Germany
1974–1980	Studied structural engineering and architecture at the University of Stuttgart
1980–1986	Post-graduate fellow in research project 'Wide-Span Lightweight Structures' at the University of Stuttgart
1981	Award for outstanding scientific achievements
1983	Fazlur R. Khan Award of the Skidmore, Owings & Merrill Foundation, N.Y.
1984	Worked for Skidmore, Owings & Merrill, Chicago
1987	PhD in Structural Engineering
1987–1991	Structural Engineer at Schlaich, Bergermann & Partner, Stuttgart
1988–1991	Teaching fellowship for 'Designing Load-Bearing Structures' at the Department of Civil Engineering of the University of Stuttgart
1989	Hubert Rüsch Prize of the German Concrete Association
1991–1995	Professor at the University of Hanover (successor to Bernd Tokarz) and Director of the Institute for Structural Design and Building Methods
1991	German Civil Engineering Award
1992	Founded his own engineering firm
1995	Professor at the University of Stuttgart (successor to Frei Otto) Director of the Institute for Lightweight Structures and of the Central Laboratory for Civil Engineering. Exhibition 'Werner Sobek – Buildings and Projects', Galerie am

An architecture that claims to formulate a mind-set appropriate to our time as well as to future generations has to be an architecture that does not take shape through the use of traditional forms and materials. It rather has to develop on the basis of integral processes of planning and organization that take into consideration present and future forms of human life. The question is not "How did we live and work until now?" but rather "How are we going to live and work in the future?" The answer to this question might not always prove perfectly true. But with respect to intellectual tenability seeking to answer this question is the only possible way.

There are few who look ahead, who have committed themselves to the advancement of the existing. For myself and for my teams in our Stuttgart and Frankfurt offices it is the only possible way.

For us, the term "engineering" never meant the simple follow-up of an architect's thoughts and the analysis of what somebody else has sketched before. For us, engineering means to bring in all the ingenuity of a multi-discipline team into the conceptual phase of the planning process from the very first second. Engineering means creativity. Engineering means to work with all the materials available on earth in such a way that each of them is used in an appropriate manner and as an integral part of the entire architectural idea. Engineering means to take advantage of all the methods developed in mechanics, mathematics and other related fields. But engineering never means only to explain how the existing things function: Engineering means to create new things and to guarantee that they function.

I met Helmut Jahn first in 1994. It took only a few meetings for us to find deep confidence in the sincerity, frankness, creativity and professionalism of the other. A deep and extraordinary collaboration and friendship developed from this. The way Helmut and I are working together

functions with a wink. We are working together on all our projects from the very first moment. Work starts on the phone, in a taxi, a restaurant or even in one of the offices. Our work is significantly characterized by a high density of thoughts each of us brings into the creative process at the same time (forget about the world around you) and by the fact that many of those thoughts belong to the discipline of the other. Helmut is discussing structural solutions as well as I contribute to architectural thoughts. It is our very special interpersonal relation that allows for this and that leads to so many highly acknowledged buildings. Some of those buildings are at the cutting edge of what one can do today, some of them are remarkably complex and of huge size. But each one of them is characterized by a more and more rigorous simplicity and a beauty resulting from this.

I met Matthias Schuler first in 1992. Matthias was born close to my hometown, in an area where many outstanding engineers grew up and where they worked for their whole life. For me it was very clear that the work of Matthias interlocked perfectly with what we were doing. I therefore introduced Matthias to Helmut who felt the same as I did. This led to a long-time cooperation between the three of us.

The approach of Matthias Schuler to building design differs somewhat from Helmut Jahn's and my work since Matthias concentrates more on innovating the energy-flow within a building, less on the forming and shaping of what will be physically built. However, of course energy-flows and the creation of comfort also condition the structural and the architectural solutions, and they influence by the physical demands its colors and its surface qualities. Therefore it is essential that everybody in our team understands what the other needs or where he wants to go to, our objective goals are the same: the achievement of a built environment for which we can take responsibility.

Werner Sobek

MATTHIAS SCHULER

BIOGRAPHY

1958	Born September 26, 1958 in Stuttgart, Germany
1987	Graduated mechanical engineer from University Stuttgart
1987–1992	Assistant researcher "Institut für Thermodynamik und Wärmetechnik", University Stuttgart; international research project on "Passive and Hybrid Solar Commercial Building" in the framework of the International Energy Agency, Department N.M. Fisch
1990	TRNSYS developer partnership with University Wisconsin, Bill Beckmann
1992	Founder of "Transsolar Energietechnik GmbH", Schwäbisch Gmünd
1993	Directing partner at Transsolar with Peter Voit and Thomas Lechner; managing director
1994	Lecture at Architectural Department Polytechnical Highschool, Biberach with Andreas Theilig
1996	Hugo Häring Price for project "Datapec Headquarter" in collaboration with Kauffmann Theilig
1998	University Stuttgart, lecture at "Institut für Baukonstruktion", Prof. Stefan Behling and "Institut für leichte Flächentragwerke", Prof. Werner Sobek
2000	Harvard University, Visiting Professor at Graduated School of Design, Design Studio with Toshiko Mori
2000	Extended partnership Transsolar with Thomas Auer, Stefan Holst and Volkmar Bleicher
2001	Harvard University, Visiting Professor at GSD, Core lecture on "Environmental Systems in Building"

The oil crisis of the seventies led to increased research for energy-saving strategies in the building sector. The reason for this was that around one third of the European energy demand was being used for the heating, lighting and cooling of buildings. As a result of these international activities in the US and Europe, simulation tools were developed and verified through comparisons with measurements. These tools allowed us to evaluate the system's behavior and compare different system solutions. By the beginning of the nineties, these tools for energy, daylighting and fluid dynamics were well known in research, but they still hardly influenced the daily design activities in the building sector. Here, steady state calculations were used to size systems and their components, leading to multiple over-sizing.

For the first five years in my profession I worked as a researcher on an international project involved with solar commercial buildings, which had been initiated by the International Energy Agency IEA. During the course of this project I learned to communicate with architects, and developed a certain sensitivity for their approach to architectural design, which is quite different from that of an engineer. With the knowledge of this potential and of the demands, I founded the climate consulting company Transsolar in 1992. By rethinking the basics of physics we seek to introduce new energy-saving and comfort-optimizing strategies during the early building design stage. By communicating with architects and other members of the design team, we can develop integrated building concepts and evaluate them by using simulation tools. Our main approach is to understand the building itself as a climate system. Optimizing building form, orientation, construction and façade systems minimizes additional demands for heating, cooling and lighting. This, in turn, leads to dramatically reduced mechanical systems and big energy savings. This aim of saving energy and optimizing comfort with reduced investment and lower operating costs, has been verified empirically in our first built projects. During this period we completed different projects with Werner Sobek and his team, most of which were in collaboration with the architects Peter Hübner and Andreas Theilig.

Getting Started

In 1994, Werner Sobek called us to ask if we were able and interested in being involved in the New International Bangkok Airport project with the architects Murphy/Jahn. Six weeks later, we met Helmut Jahn in Berlin and presented our first concept proposals and simulation results to him. In the end, we were chosen to join the team. During the following months we worked with Helmut and Werner to develop an integrated solution for the building envelope and mechanical system that would emphasize the concept of an airport that relied on natural lighting during the daytime. The theoretical concept for the lightweight building shell as well as the feasibility discussions in Bangkok with the client and his consultants were only minor problems; the major challenge consisted in procuring suitable building materials, since they were not available as end products and thus had to be constructed from components. In collaboration with the acoustics expert Rainer Blum, a two-year phase of development led to a first pricing and therefore the reliability of the triple layer membrane construction. Our final concept cut the cooling peak for the entire airport by 40% as compared to a standard solution, thus we not only saved a remarkable amount in investment costs but also reduced the annual energy demand of operations by one third.

The final membrane roof solution for the Bangkok Airport combines the architectural aesthetics of a light and translucent skin with the structural simplicity of minimal material input to meet the thermal and acoustic demands. None of us could have come up with this solution on our own.

Teamwork

What I found most fascinating was that an internationally renown architect like Helmut Jahn, who had built numerous projects all over the world, was open-minded enough to listen to young engineers and that he took a chance in strengthening his design approach by taking into account physical aspects already in early design phases. We did not see eye to eye on every subject and even today we choose to disagree on the topic of the efficiency and acceptance of external shading devices. But by not accepting the easiest solution, Helmut Jahn and his architects urged us to come up with new ones. Together with Werner Sobek, whose sensitivity and understanding goes far beyond mere structure and who is interested in the structural and energy aspects of building shells, our team covers nearly all aspects of building design. Through teamwork and experience, we at Transsolar have gained the insight that pure design criteria and convincing energy concepts will be taken seriously. This gives us the freedom to think in terms limited only by physical impossibilities and the assurance that if a concept works, the other two partners will support it against criticism with their full weight and profession.

Nowadays we – the architects Murphy/Jahn, Werner Sobek Ingenieure and Transsolar Energietechnik – collaborate with the knowledge of the other partners' basic strategies, predilections and weak points, and we are very effective in developing and fixing new building concepts. Nevertheless, the confrontation between the architectural visions and the engineering limits drive us to develop new solutions. Not every component for each new project has to be developed from scratch, but it is re-examined and re-assessed in respect to necessity and dimension on a case by case basis. On the other hand, basic strategies do not need to be discussed each time anew. Acknowledgement for realized projects has a direct influence on those still in progress.

In addition to a good design team, "new" and "cutting edge" solutions also require a client who personally identifies with the project and is willing to take the risk of doing something new

outside of the "accepted rules of technique". A project like Bayer or Deutsche Post could never have been built with anonymous clients. The strong and rapid developments in building material technologies is not always mirrored in real building construction. It is the common consensus of the group that we must continuously push for further advancements by striving to apply the newest developments in our projects.

Challenges and Visions

Our challenge in respect to teamwork is to coordinate the approaches for transparency, sustainability and user comfort.

The wish for building transparency – nowadays supported by the strong developments in the glass industry related to thermal and solar protection with optimized daylighting transmission – is to push for new solutions in façade systems, including solar and glare protection demand.
Simplification and combined use are a driving force that can be tapped by the broad understanding afforded by our three disciplines.

Buildings should not been built for the next few years only, but for at least 30-50 years. It is important to consider a great flexibility for further kinds of use and developing systems. Reuse must have priority over recycling, because the embedded energy cannot be used to recycle the building components, which is generally a down-cycling for a lower-ranked use.

Most importantly, we are building buildings for people to work and live in, thus the occupants' comfort – related to thermal, visual and acoustic comfort – has to be our goal, while keeping the input of materials and energy to build and run the facility as low as possible. And considering the fact that we have the technical preconditions, at least for the majority of climates, my vision is to construct self-sustaining buildings that heat, ventilate and cool themselves without using an external energy input and without producing enormous amounts of CO_2 every day.   Matthias Schuler

PRINCIPAL FINANCIAL GROUP

Des Moines, Iowa
Design 1993/Completion 1996
Client: Principal Mutual Life Insurance
Helmut Jahn

The design of this building started in 1993 and signaled a return to a more technical approach, after the formal and stylistic attempts of the 80's and early 90's.

The project expands Principal's downtown campus in Des Moines to the north and creates a large plaza between the original headquarters and the new structure. A louvered trellis creates a transitional forecourt to the gate through the building, accommodating entry and connection to planned future developments to the north.

Within this construct the buildings' components are simple metal and glass structures, like the sky-bridge connecting to the existing headquarter, the glass bridge crossing the gate, the trellis creating the forecourt, the open stairs at the exterior and interior, and the different types of curtain walls responding to different building and urban conditions.

In the implementation of the building it became obvious, that the demand for simple, straightforward glass- and steel construction was very taxing on the engineering profession and the construction industry, which had become somewhat complacent in the 'post-modern' times of the 80's and forgotten about the principals of technical design and construction due to a lack of challenge by the architects and owners.

GROUND LEVEL

REEDY CREEK IMPROVEMENT DISTRICT

Buena Vista, Florida
Design 1995/Completion 1997
Client: Disney Development Co.
Reedy Creek Improvement District
Helmut Jahn

The building houses the headquarters of the
Reedy Creek Improvement District and central-
izes the agency functions for the Walt Disney
companies large Orlando developments. Thus it
projects a neutral identity in difference to the
other 'themed' projects.

A simple square plan is chamfered at the corners to create on two sides ascending skylights
and on the other two sides sloped overhangs.
The building is clad with floor-to-floor glass
walls and completed at the corners with trellis
structures with growing vines, which outline
the original cubic composition and connect the
building to the lush landscape.

The wall is double glazed with coated heat reflective glass and interior horizontal blinds. Due
to its compact shape the wall area is minimal-
ized and the building inherently energy efficient
with maximum daylight.

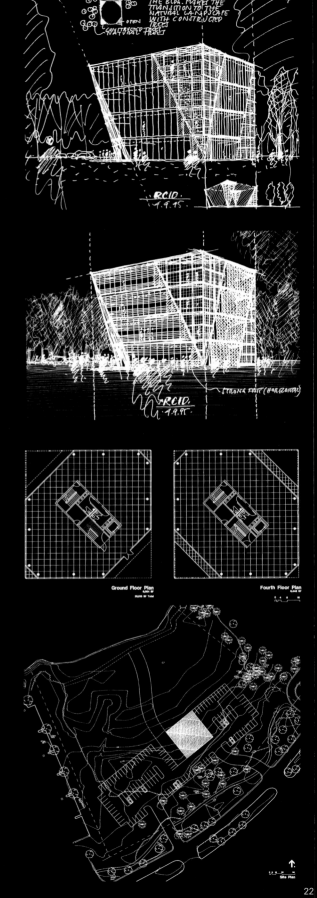

South Elevation

East Elevation

North Elevation

West Elevation

23

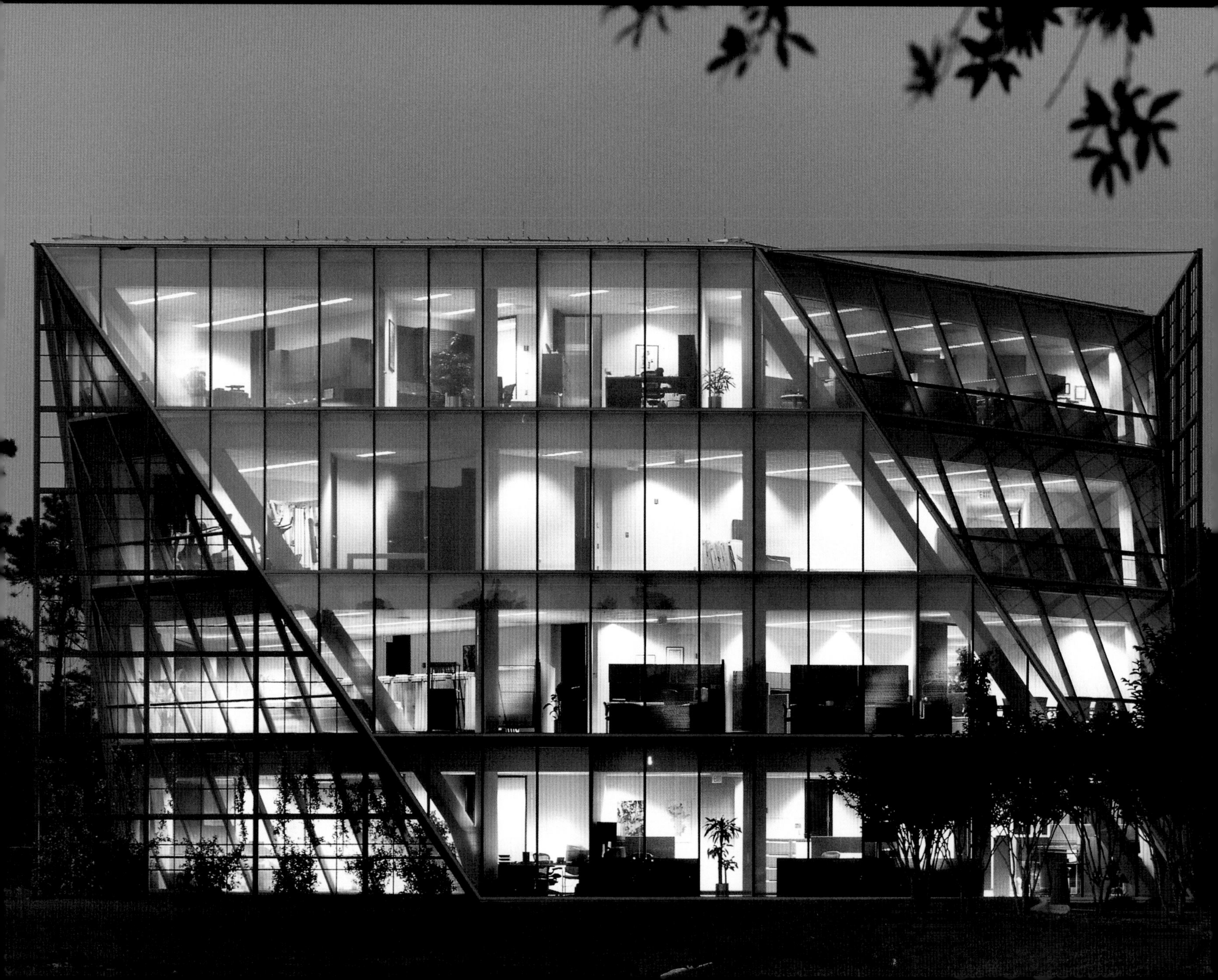

CHARLEMAGNE – EUROPEAN UNION

Bruxelles, Belgium
Design 1994/Completion 1998
Client: S.A. Cofinimmo N.V.
Helmut Jahn/Werner Sobek
Associate Architect: Bureau d'Architecture
Henri Montois, S.A. Bureau Paul Noel

This project is the renovation of an existing building built in 1968. Like so many of the structures of this period, the building was unresponsive, almost hostile to its city context.

By carefully subtracting or adding from its original volume and cladding the building with a light, transparent glass wall, it becomes more engaging with its environs. By running the glass walls beyond its volume, also a response to the major street in front of it, the visual potential of glass is exploited and at times the boundaries of the building become 'blurred'. At its curved side the open courts and 'glass beams' merge into the fabric of the adjacent historic city.

While working on Sony Center and Bangkok airport with Werner Sobek, the façades here became the prototype for Sony and subsequent projects.

The glass fins are load bearing for life-load-conditions and located either outside or inside the skin surface. At the projecting screens they are held by filigree metal structures. Fire regulations in Brussels did not allow for a floor-to-floor glass wall, thus 0.8 m stainless steel panels were placed behind glass panels or flush with the glazing at the slab edges.

The Auditorium- and conference wing use point supported glass mounted to special steel structures.

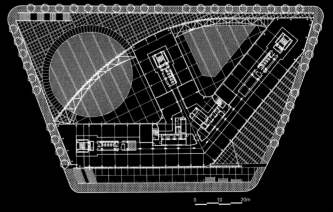

3 PARTIAL ELEVATION

1 PARTIAL

2 PARTIAL PLAN

1a PARTIAL

JC DECAUX BUS SHELTER

Prototype
Design 1997/Completion 1998
Client: JC Decaux
Helmut Jahn/Werner Sobek

The design manifests itself as a minimal and technical expression in structural glass. With its aspects of transparency, reflection, opacity and refraction, the shelter becomes a crystal in the urban environment. The design establishes a contrast with the typical existing city-fabric. Without competition old and new reinforce each other and keep their own identities.

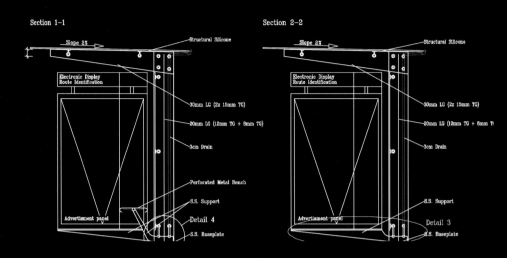

Section 1-1

Slope 2%
Structural Silicone
Electronic Display
Route Identification
30mm LG (2x 15mm TG)
20mm LG (12mm TG + 8mm TG)
3cm Drain
Perforated Metal Bench
S.S. Support
Advertisment panel
Detail 4
S.S. Baseplate

Section 2-2

Slope 2%
Structural Silicone
Electronic Display
Route Identification
30mm LG (2x 15mm TG)
20mm LG (12mm TG + 8mm T
3cm Drain
S.S. Support
Advertisment panel
Detail 3
S.S. Baseplate

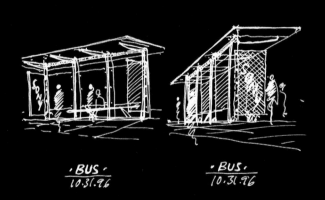

· BUS ·
10.31.96

· BUS ·
10.31.96

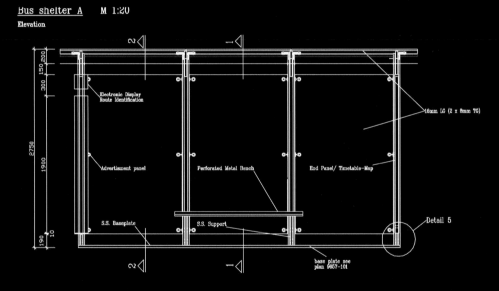

Bus shelter A   M 1:20
Elevation

Electronic Display
Route Identification
Advertisment panel
Perforated Metal Bench
End Panel/ Timetable-Map
16mm LG (2 x 8mm TG)
Detail 5
S.S. Baseplate
S.S. Support
base plate see
plan 9657-101

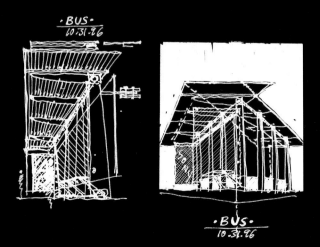

· BUS ·
10.31.96

· BUS ·
10.31.96

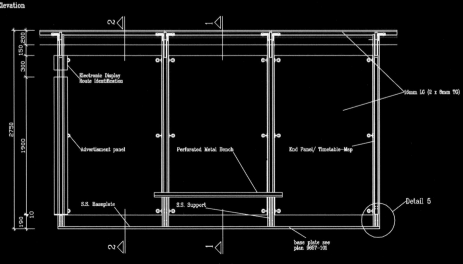

Bus shelter A   M 1:20
Elevation

Electronic Display
Route Identification
Advertisment panel
Perforated Metal Bench
End Panel/ Timetable-Map
16mm LG (2 x 8mm TG)
Detail 5
S.S. Baseplate
S.S. Support
base plate see
plan 9657-101

MUNICH AIRPORT CENTER

Munich, Germany
Design 1990/Completion 1999
Client: Flughafen München GmbH; MFG,
Delta KG; ALBA GmbH
Helmut Jahn/Ove Arup + Partners/
Werner Sobek

KEMPINSKI HOTEL

Munich, Germany
Design 1989/Completion 1994
Client: Flughafen München GmbH
Helmut Jahn/Jörg Schlaich

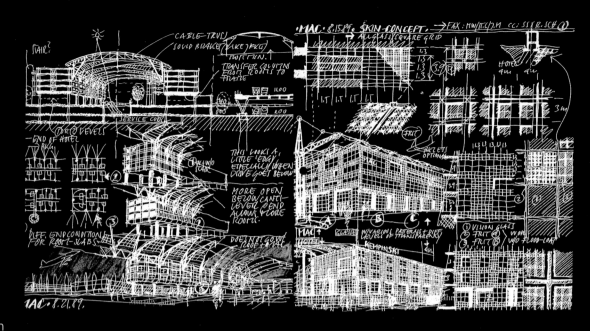

The projects at the Munich Airport started in 1988. Starting with the Masterplan and Kempinski Hotel and recently completed Munich Airport Center (MAC) they span over 11 years. In 1998, we competed for Terminal 2 which closes the Forum of the MAC to the east. Though we were not successful, our proposal, however, informed, after several steps in the competition process, the built solution, which will go a further step towards making the commercial zone of the airport a city outside the city.

The Airport City was the idea of the original masterplan prepared by us in 1988 and up-dated in 2001. This new plan adds 350 rooms to the Kempinski Hotel and a Conference Center north of the Kempinski Hotel garden. We are implementing this plan now, according to the principles of an integrated architecture/engineering approach.

The design of the buildings is guided by the recognition that today's airports are more than transportation hubs. They become 'cities outside cities', a combination of mall and airport. The Forum of the MAC becomes the airport-city's central square, the first and last impression of the city and the region.

The roofs are the parts, which create the image. At the Kempinski Hotel we worked with Jörg Schlaich and at the MAC with Ove Arup + Part-

ners. Special glass structures are part of the hotel and the MAC, later done with Werner Sobek.

The roofs create covered open or closed rooms, which together with the open spaces in between draw the surrounding landscape into the architecture. Conceptually, the normal division

between exterior and interior space is broken down and a transition is made from high technology to nature. The airport is never opposed to the natural world, but strives to complement it.

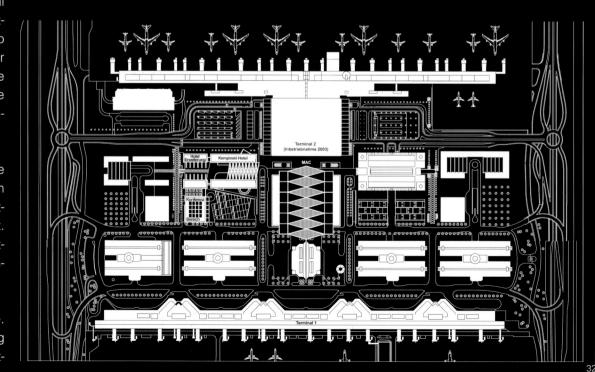

TEILANSICHT

TEILGRUDRISS

9 DETAIL

8 DETAIL

3 SCHNITT

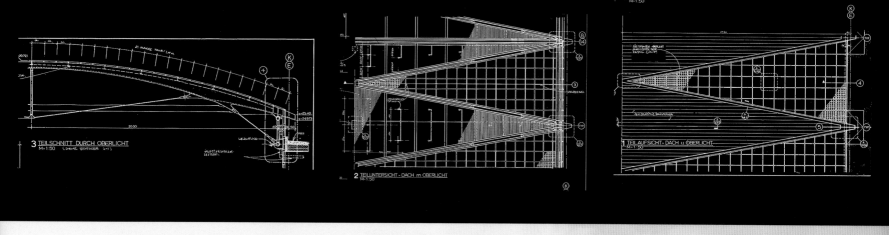

3 TEILSCHNITT DURCH OBERLICHT
M = 1:50

2 TEILUNTERSICHT - DACH m OBERLICHT
M = 1:50

1 TEILAUFSICHT - DACH u OBERLICHT
M = 1:50

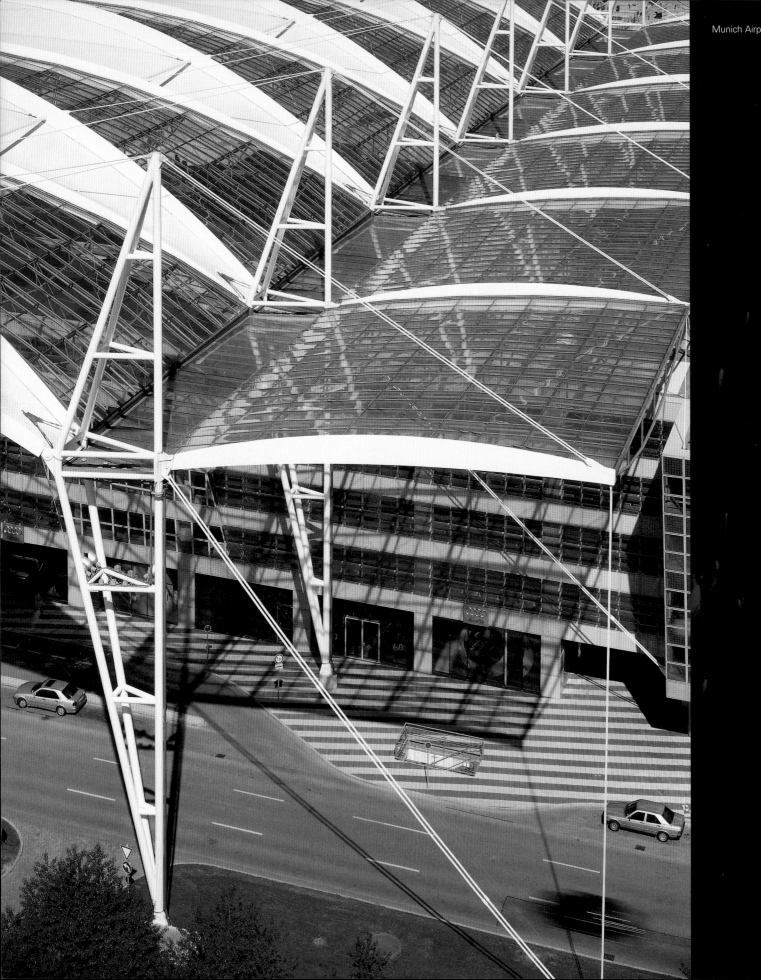

SONY CENTER

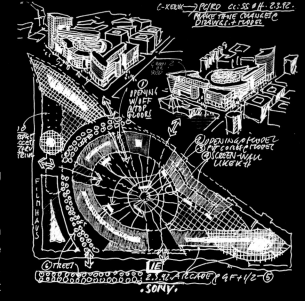

Berlin, Germany
Design 1993/Completion 2000
Client: Sony with its Partners
TishmanSpeyer Properties and Kajima
Helmut Jahn/Ove Arup + Partners/
Werner Sobek

Sony Center started with a competition in the summer of 1992. We worked with Ove Arup + Partners as structural engineering consultant, primarily on the Forum roof. When the project, after a slow period, came into full swing in 1994, Werner Sobek was added to the team to design the special structures in steel and glass. He further consulted on the principles of an integrated architecture/engineering approach, which we both had become very interested in at that time.

Sony does not only represent an urban idea, but stands for a technical vision and order and the creation of an 'envelope' for a new social interaction of our time. The external 'real city' is contrasted by the internal 'virtual city'.

In working with Werner Sobek, Ove Arup and the local engineers of BGS and IGH the constructional concept evolved as an application of a series of components. Structure, enclosure and the conditioning system were developed according to building configuration, function, use and comfort. It was the client's wish to make the buildings' comfort be generated primarily by technical systems. We were, however, successful in maximizing natural resources like daylight and optional natural ventilation. Through the configuration of the façades at the office/apartment buildings, especially at the Forum, the interaction with the outside is maxi-mized and through their transparency the buildings engage with the life of the city.

The Forum roof creates a climate-shift and allows for greatly expanded use. But purposely it does not totally eliminate the effects of rain, snow and wind to still give the feeling of being outdoors and within the public realm.

Sony Center became a very pivotal project in our work. The previous individual pursuits came together to become a more integrated whole. Not being just one building, but a complex that becomes part of the city, it contributes to the dialog about Berlin's reconstruction and promotes an aesthetic of construction. It opened the way for subsequent projects to deal with issues like decreasing the use of technical equipment, increasing the use of natural resources and improving comfort with less energy.

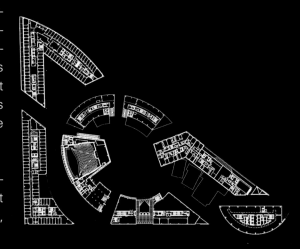

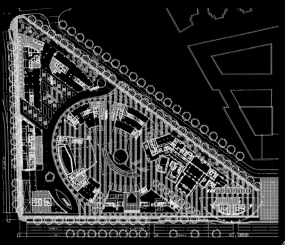

FRIT CHANGES FROM
HEAVEY TO CLEAR — CLEAR

FABRIC
GLASS — TOP ROOF

ELEV ·d
RAMP T
OLUVUS

ROOF BOTTOL

UK Decken-
verkleidung

Detail 4

2xd=24

2xd=24

2xd=24

2xd=24

2xd=24

2xd=24

45°

45°

2000

2xd=24

2xd=24

2xd=24

oberste Glasscheibe

ESPLANADE

Re

Bellevuestraße 1

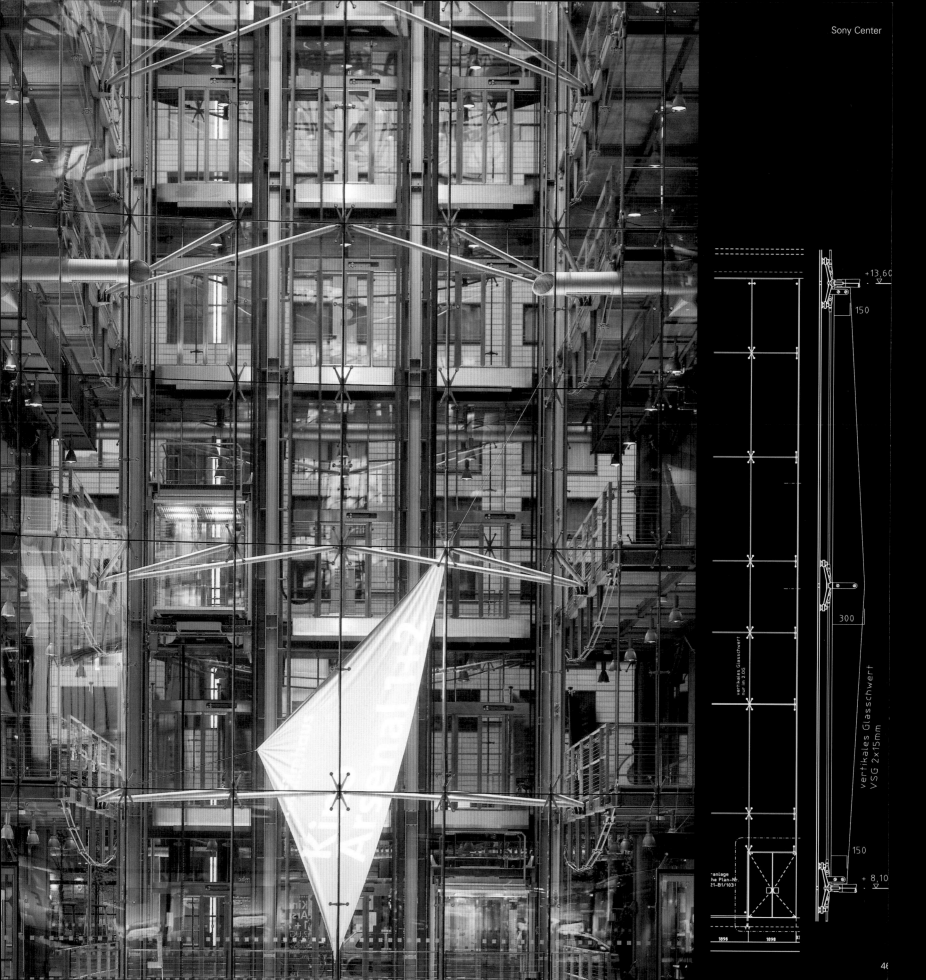

+13,60

150

vertikales Glasschwert
nur im 2.OG

300

vertikales Glasschwert
VSG 2x15mm

150

+ 8,10

-anlage
-he Plan-Nr.
21-B1/103

1898   1898

Detail 1 M=1:10
Horizontalbinder

Bei der Nordfassade besteht der
Horizontalbinder im Penthouse aus
Zugstäben Ø 34.
Die darunterliegenden Horizontal-
binder bestehen aus Zugstäben
Ø 28.
Bei der Südfassade besteht
der Horizontalbinder im 10.OG
aus Zugstäben Ø 34.
Die darunterliegenden Horizontal-
binder bestehen aus Zugstäben
Ø 28.

Schnitt a-a

vertikale Ab-
spannung Ø
12

Ø 48,3x4,0

Ø 28 bzw.
Ø 34

Ø 16

Aufsicht b-b

Ø 28 bzw.
Ø 34

Ø 28 bzw.
Ø 34

vertikale Ab-
spannung Ø
12

Ø 48,3x4,0

Ø 28 bzw.
Ø 34

Ø 28 bzw.
Ø 34

Ø 28 bzw.
Ø 34

le Ab-
ng Ø 8

Ø 48,3x4,0

Ø 28 bzw.
Ø 34

Ø 48.3×4.0

Detail 4

Detail

Detail 7

Gelenk

VK Fassade

Ø 48.3×2.9

Ø 48.3×4.0

1250   1100

Ø 48.3×4.0

Ø 28   Ø 28

Ø 12   Ø 8

Ø 48.3×4.0

Detail 8

Gelenk

Detail 4

1 ELEVATION

2 PLAN

3 SECTION

PLAN AT PARAPET

PLAN AT GLAZING

1 ELEVATION

3 SECTION

1 ELEVATION

FLUGHAFEN KÖLN/BONN

Design 1992/Completion 2000
Client: Flughafen Köln/Bonn GmbH
Helmut Jahn/Werner Sobek/
Ove Arup + Partners

In 1992 an international competition lead to Murphy/Jahn's commission for Terminal 2, the 2-level Roadway structure, Parkhaus 2 and 3 and an underground Railstation. Terminal 2 and the parking structures are now complete and the station is under construction. The competition team with Ove Arup + Partners was expanded with Werner Sobek, who did the terminal's façades and the special structures of the garage and the roof of the train station.

Whereas the existing building is of concrete and solid, the new building is constructed of prefabricated steel and glass components on an exposed concrete substructure, creating a very light and transparent appearance.

The roof consists of panels, so-called cells, which are placed onto the folded plate trusses with simple bolted connections and waterproof joint seals. The cells are designed to fulfill various functions such as: light transmission, weather barrier, exterior heat absorption, interior heat absorption, acoustic dampening and absorption, and smoke ventilation. This is the first step in a series of buildings, which aim to create a skin with self-adapting qualities by combining different types of cells. Then a building's roof or façade are no longer a product with constant properties but can become the technical equivalent of the biological skin.

The façade is a lightweight cable-supported steel and glass structure. The insulating glass panels are held by "spiders" at their joints. Similar advanced lightweight and glass technologies are applied to the glass railings, elevators, fixed and moveable jet bridges, and glass floors and stairs.

Conditioned air is supplied to the departure hall

via freestanding air columns integrated into the steel trees supporting the roof.

The parking structures are clad on the long sides with stretched panels of stainless steel mesh. Based on lighting conditions their appearance varies from opaque to transparent, generating wonderful effects, while passing through it, or driving by it. The large floor plates are punctuated by light courts with walls of cable-nets with vines to achieve natural ventilation and provide daylight.

The underground 4-track station is covered by a slightly arched glass roof, supported by steel pipes, which projects over its 200 m length out of the ground.

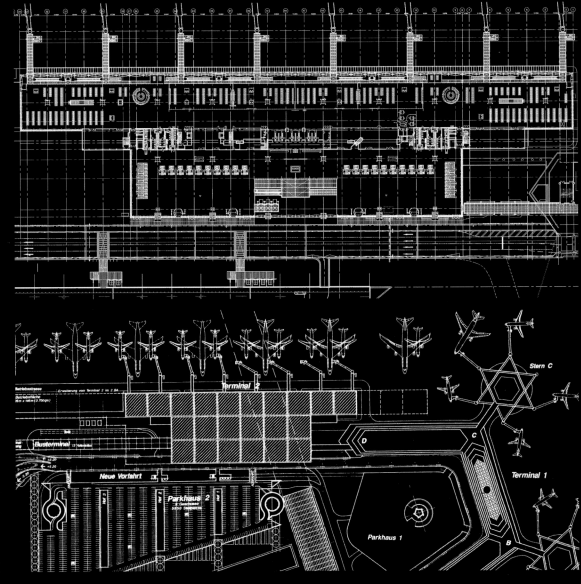

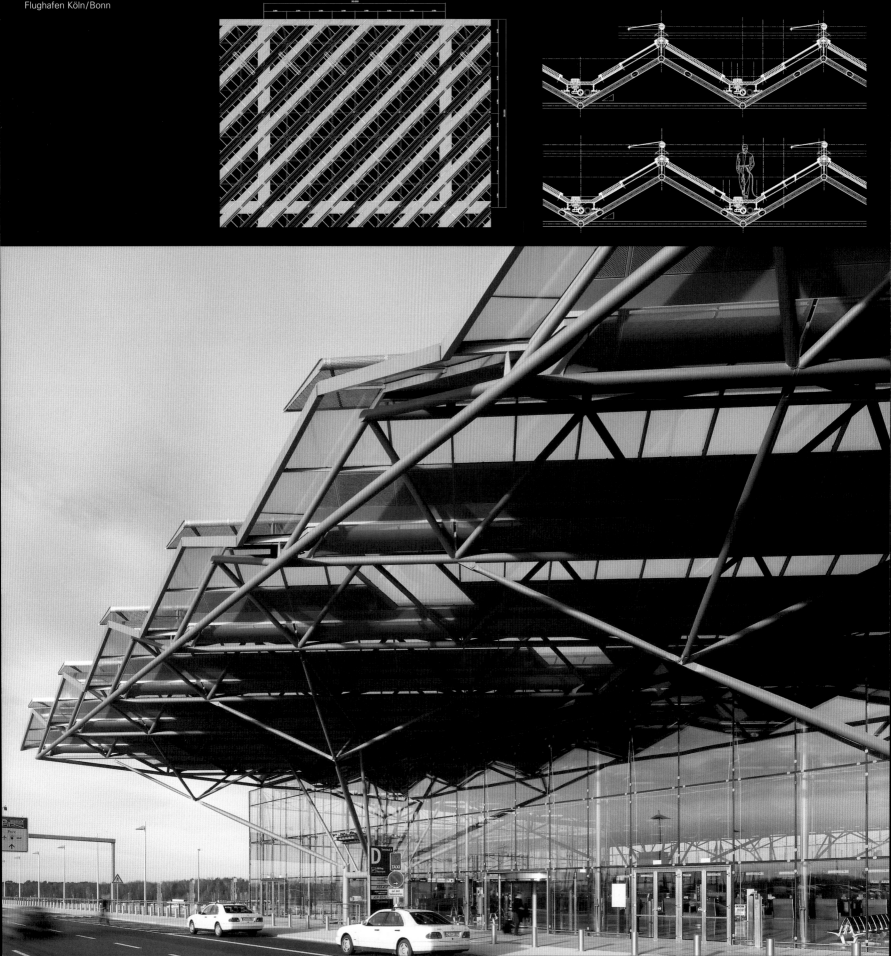

Flughafen Köln/Bonn

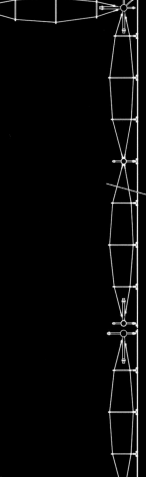

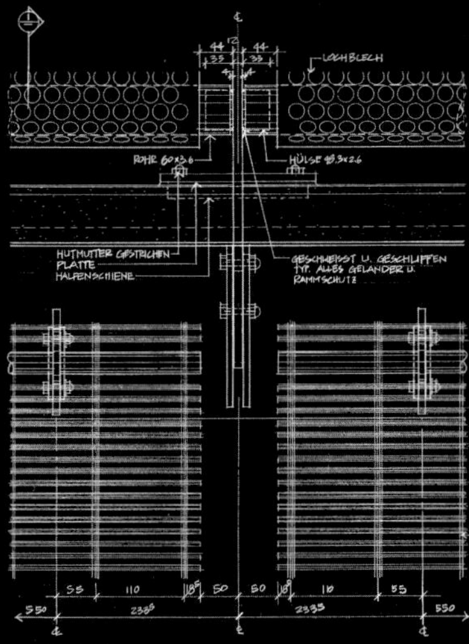

4 ANSICHT

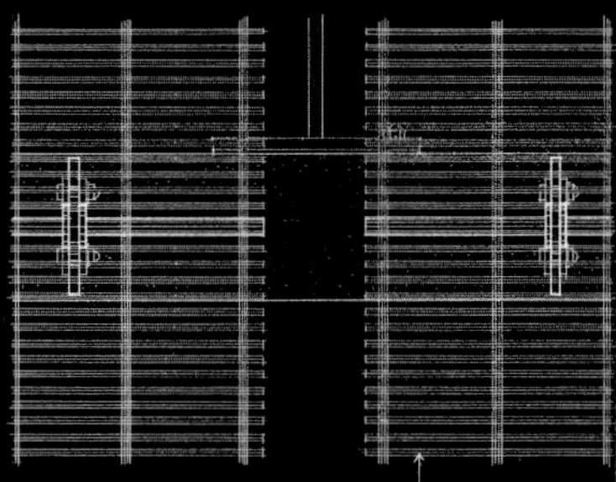

5 ANSICHT

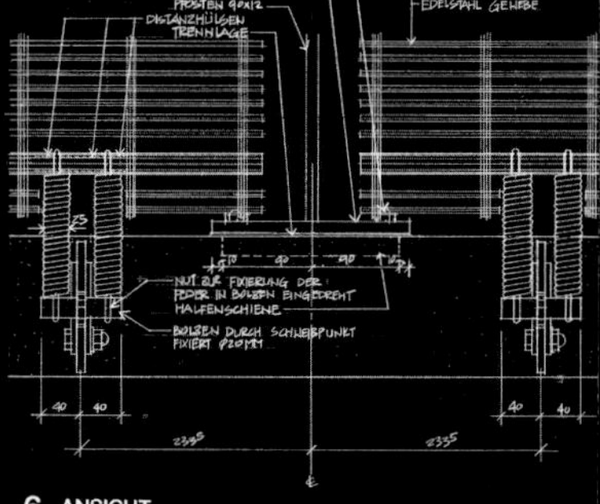

6 ANSICHT

NEUES KRANZLER ECK

Berlin, Germany
Design 1992/Completion 2001
Client: DIFA Deutsche Immobilien Fonds AG
Helmut Jahn/Werner Sobek

The project started in 1988, the year before the Berlin Wall came down. In an invited competition we proposed a 114 m Tower, which replaced all the existing buildings on the site, as a statement for a new Berlin.

It was not until 1992, when Victoria Versicherung resumed the project. By that time the planning attitude in Berlin had changed. Hans Stimmann, the Senatsbaudirektor, advocated a policy of 'critical reconstruction' with the goal of recreating the character of the traditional European City in a new way.

After a series of alternative design studies a scheme was jointly chosen with the City. Victoria then sold the project to DIFA, which completed it. This scheme was based on keeping the existing landmarked buildings built in 1957 by Hans Dustmann and completing the original plan with a tower-slab stretching from Kurfürstendamm to Kantstraße.

The energy-comfort concept, developed with Brandi Consult, makes a breakthrough. A heating/cooling panel at the perimeter controls the façades' energy-transmission in winter and summer. Basic conditioning is provided by a displacement system of conditioned air from the floor. Exhaust air is returned through the corridors. Sprinklers, electrical and communication distribution are integrated into the raised, accessible floor. Thus no suspended ceilings are needed and the floor-to-ceiling height is increased. The displacement system follows natural physical principles of cold air rising as it heats up on people and equipment.

The experience on Sony helped to simplify and optimize the glass structures. Single glass fins, instead of double-fins and carbon-fiber frames replace the conventional metal-sash at the operable windows. The triangular glass point representing the 'City Sign' is suspended from the buildings' concrete structure and contains a dynamic light sculpture by Yann Kersalé. The static counter-point to this piece is the illuminated glass-canopy covering the passage from Kurfürstendamm to Kantstraße. The split Volière is the centerpiece of the court and completes the composition with the buildings Loggia and Gate.

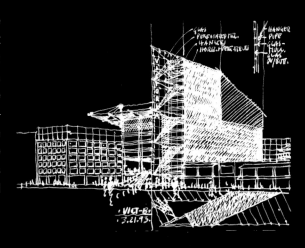

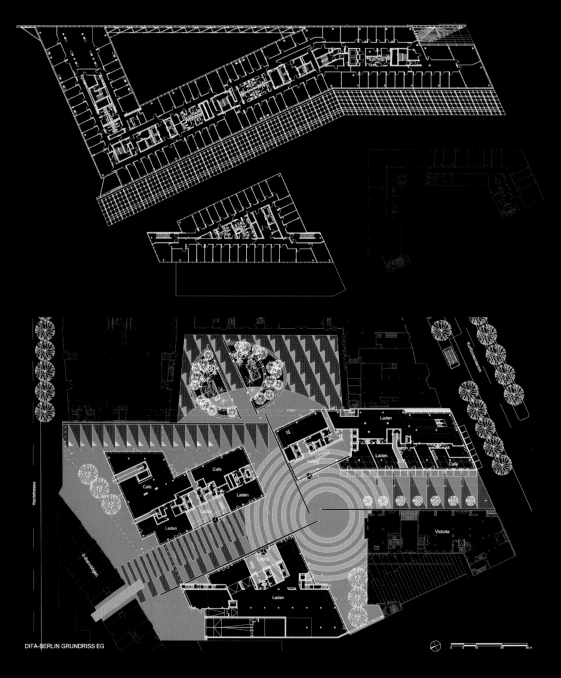

DIFA-BERLIN GRUNDRISS EG

GÖRTZ 17

GÖRTZ 17

ANSICHT

GRUNDRISS

SCHNITT

DECKENSPIEGEL

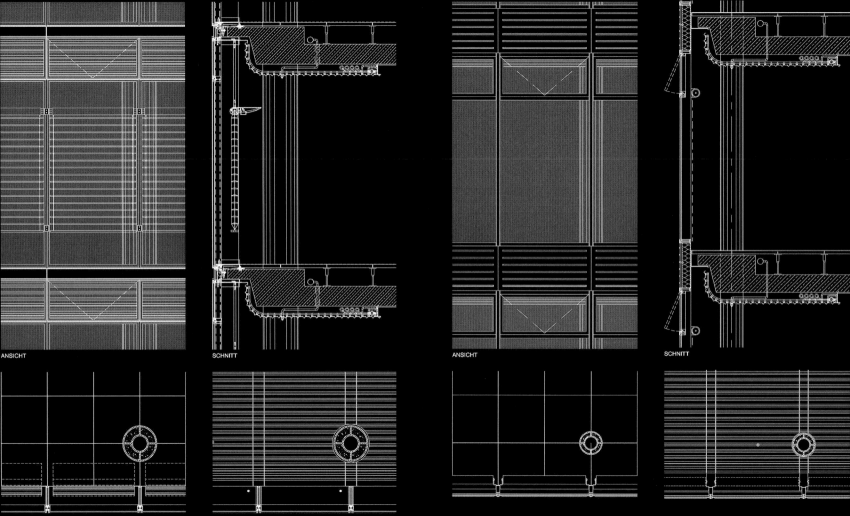

ANSICHT

SCHNITT

ANSICHT

SCHNITT

HA•LO HEADQUARTERS
Niles, Illinois
Design 1998/Completion 2001
Client: CenterPoint Properties
Helmut Jahn/Werner Sobek

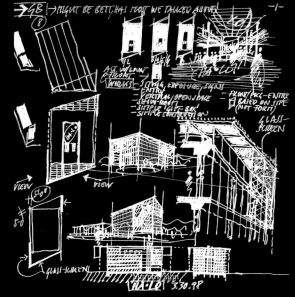

While doing all these overseas projects, much of our American work had dried up. Potential clients were not interested in this type of work or afraid of its demanding precision or its uncertain effect on the user or tenant. Engineers and contractors were too complacent and busy with the 'post-modern' routine of the time. Thinking forward, inventing, yes, taking some chances was not popular.

Then I met Louis Weissbach, who founded HA•LO out of the trunk of his car and made it the most successful promotional product company in the United States. He was ready for something different. We designed and built a building which transferred some of the European know-how to the United States and adapted it to the American conventions. Unfortunately HA•LO, which grew rapidly through acquisitions, fell victim to the internet-craze and went through a lot of corporate upheaval and never finished the building as designed and ultimately moved out in a cost-cutting move. Fortunately, the building has been acquired now by Shure, a leading maker of microphones which have been used, among many others, from Elvis Presley to Jack Kennedy.

The components used were all previously developed in our European projects and introduced to the American market. Werner Sobek, who did all the special steel and glass structures adapted the systems to the available technologies. The façade, including some special glass-fin-supported walls, same for the domed skylight, the horizontal and vertical screens and the atrium structures for stairs, elevators, hallways and railings are all generated by structural and physical necessity and show this in their aesthetic.

All services are supplied through an accessible raised floor. The displacement air-system creates superior comfort and allows elimination of suspended ceilings thereby increasing the room height in the large open office areas.

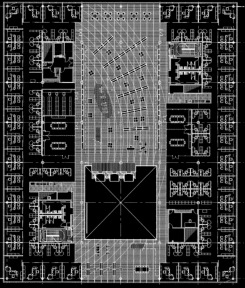

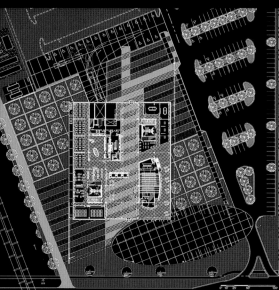

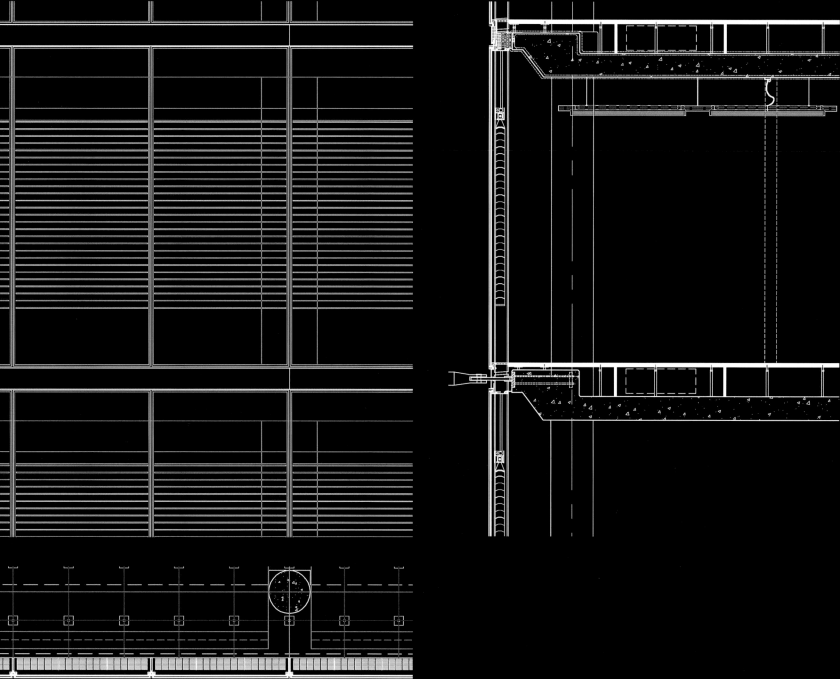

IMPERIAL BANK TOWER RENOVATION

Costa Mesa, California
Design 1998/Completion 2000
Client: C.J. Segerstrom & Sons
Helmut Jahn

With South Coast Plaza, Henry Segerstrom and his family have created a unique development combining offices, retail and cultural facilities and art in Orange County, California. Imperial Bank Tower, one of the earlier buildings, needed to be renovated to bring it up to the standards of the new structures and integrate it with the new urban patterns.

The new lobby attempts to resolve the creation of place with the facilitation of passage. Its glazed vault is extended with louvered wings, defining the space to the exterior and announcing the new image. The illumination at night further reinforces space, form and the celebratory processions towards the cultural facilities.

Light steel and cable construction supports the point glazing. The cumulative movement is accommodated at each silicone joint, eliminating the need for a special seismic joint between the connected buildings. The glazing at the top of the vault is coated with a 70 % opaque frit and a pyrolite low-E coating to reduce solar heat gain.

The space is tempered by a radiant, cooled granite floor and a displacement air system.

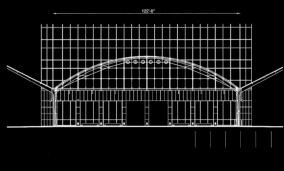

Town Center Drive

Energy Concept

1 70 % Opaque frit and high performance pyrolitic low-E coating on low iron glass to reflect heat and maximize visibility.

1A 30 % frit to sidewall glass

2 Displacement air system through bench doffusers

3 Existing construction slab integrated radiant cooling

4 Gravity dampers exhaust heated displaced air

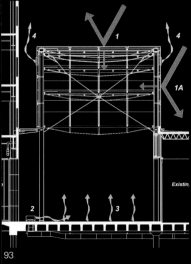

Existin,

GALERIA KAUFHOF

Chemnitz, Germany
Design 1998 / Completion 2002
Client: METRO plus Grundstücksvermietungs-
gesellschaft mbH & Co. Objekt Chemnitz KG
Helmut Jahn / Werner Sobek / Matthias Schuler

This project offered two challenges. First, we dealt with a new building-type, compared to the previous office, hotel, apartment or transportation center related projects. Second, this project in the town-center of Chemnitz constituted a piece of urban repair, to restore the Neumarkt and give again urbanity and scale to an area, where the Communist regime had left a vast, urban wasteland.

The idea was to make a totally glazed store, where display of products and integrated signage create an urban scenography, which is extended to the roofs of the adjacent Central Station and the canopies to and from the parking garage, which are lit at night by Yann Kersalé's lighting-art. The building becomes a transparent "Stadt Pavillion" with internal luminosity, especially at night.

In its systems and parts the building strives for maximum technical integration. The insulated glass panels run like a taut membrane in front of the slab-edges. The glass is point-held through their joints, with added cables and horizontal glass-fins at those conditions, where slabs do not exist. Stretched metal screens enclose the parking garage and define the edge of the cantilevered structure at the roof, changing between transparency and an opaque surface.

Air is supplied from below and exhausted to the top through ducts around the columns, keeping their sizes constant at all levels, reducing obstructions in the sales spaces to a minimum and thus eliminating horizontal duct-distribution, offering higher room heights.

The Galeria Kaufhof is a high-tech loft, technically sophisticated and highly controlled. It was made possible by an enlightened cooperation with the City of Chemnitz and the Kaufhof/Metro Organization.

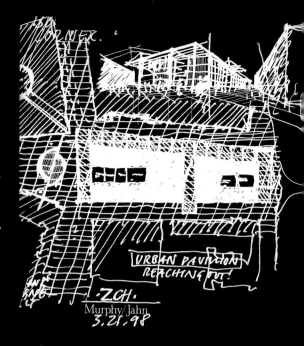

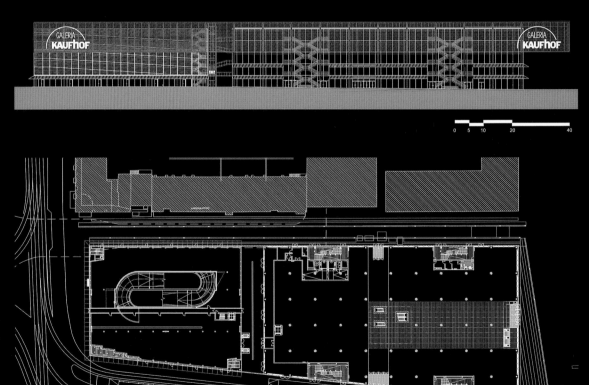

Galeria Kaufhof

OFFICE 21

Sulzbach, Germany
Design 1998
Client: Joachim Müller
Helmut Jahn/Werner Sobek/Matthias Schuler

Office 21 is the first project, after Sony and
Neues Kranzler Eck in Berlin, which dealt with
improving the comfort of buildings by using
more natural resources and with resulting less
technical equipment to become more energy-
efficient.

Originally designed for Accenture as a tenant,
the requirement was for flexibility to accommodate individual, combi, and open group offices.

To achieve the comfort goals in the fully glazed
building the façade has operable windows and
was triple glazed and internally controlled by
suspended heating and cooling panels. The
south-east and south-west exposures were
shaded by fixed glass-louvers. Internally air was
supplied by a low velocity displacements system in the raised floor, which also allowed for
the distribution of electrical- and communication services.

The central features of the building were a win-
tergarden facing south and a covered loggia facing north serving as spaces for entry and events
and connecting to the landscape.

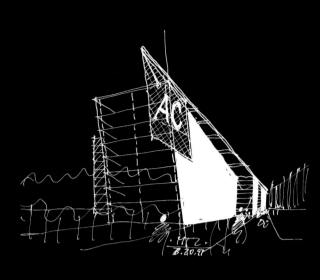

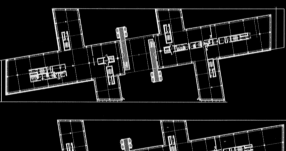

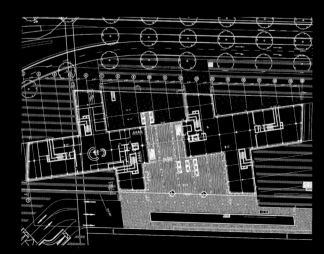

ILLINOIS INSTITUTE OF TECHNOLOGY
CAMPUS CENTER

Chicago, Illinois
Competition 1998
Client: Illinois Institute of Technology
Helmut Jahn/Werner Sobek/Matthias Schuler

This is the first project in its central core since the Mies-Campus was expanded in the late 50's and 60's by buildings of Walter Netsch and Myron Goldsmith, along the lines of the 'Miesian Principles'.

Together with Werner Sobek and Matthias Schuler we used this competition project to challenge ourselves and to make a statement about how architecture today could build from these principles and use the latest knowledge about science and technology to 'oppose' and relate to Mies.

The building expands the campus to the east, dealing with IIT's north-south obstacles of State Street and the elevated train tracks. The matrix of the plan sets boundaries and establishes linkages where appropriate.

The building is a 'Kit of Parts'. The grid mesh of the roof allows the columns' spacing to deviate, where necessary, from its regular 30' x 30' grid. It supports the so-called cells. All of them have the same size and the same edge detailing. This allows them to be placed, removed or exchanged easily by simply opening bolt connections and replacing the waterproof sealant. Each cell is designed to fulfill a limited set of functions such as variable light transmission, exterior heat absorption, interior heat absorption, solar energy conservation by photovoltaic, variable ventilation and acoustic dampening and absorption.

Though not successful here, the Campus Center project became an incubator or for subsequent projects, which embraced these ideas.

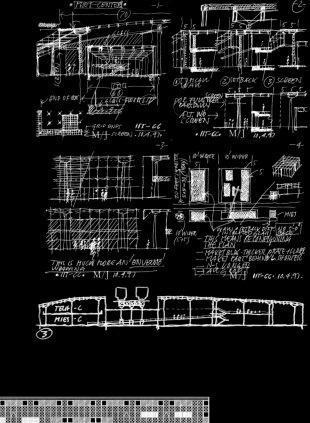

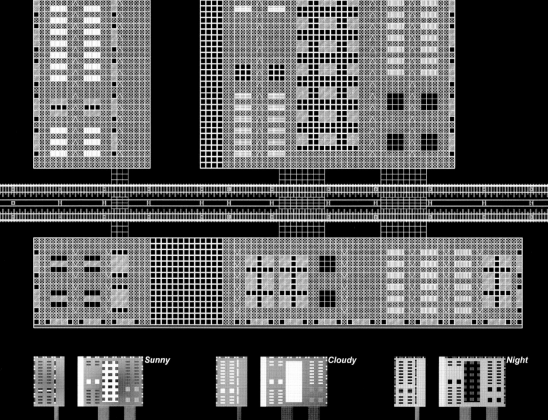

Sunny   Cloudy   Night

System detail

SYSTEM

CELLS

MESH GRID

FLOOR TRAY

ENERGY SLAB

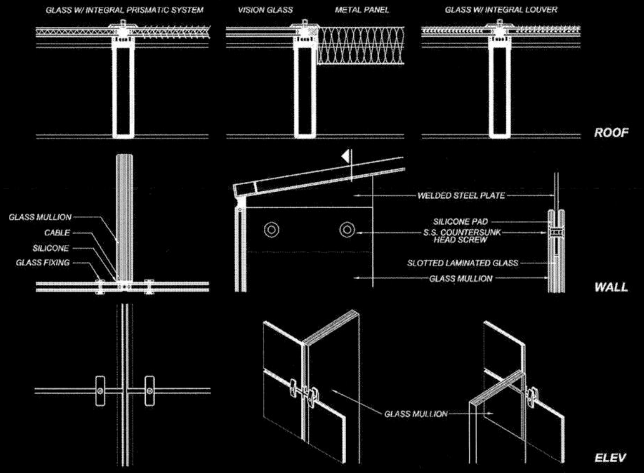

GLASS W/ INTEGRAL PRISMATIC SYSTEM   VISION GLASS   METAL PANEL   GLASS W/ INTEGRAL LOUVER

ROOF

GLASS MULLION
CABLE
SILICONE
GLASS FIXING

WELDED STEEL PLATE
SILICONE PAD
S.S. COUNTERSUNK
HEAD SCREW
SLOTTED LAMINATED GLASS
GLASS MULLION

WALL

GLASS MULLION

ELEV

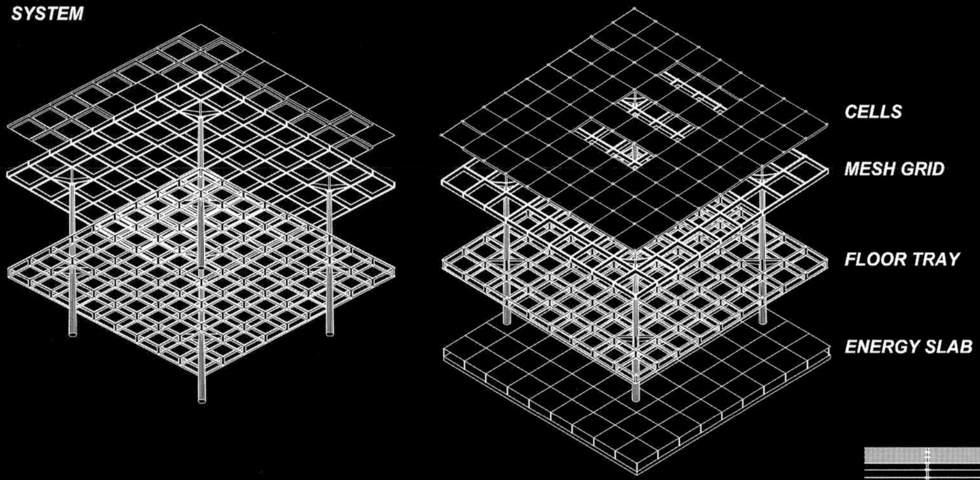

SECTIONS

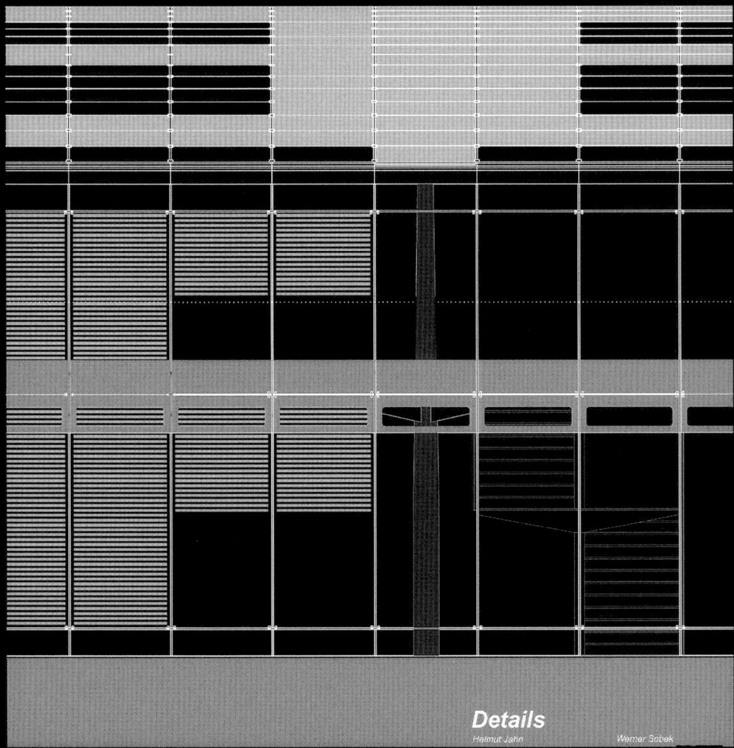

Details

Helmut Jahn   Werner Sobek

SECTION RETAIL

95°F
SHADING
83°F
78°F
74°F
74°F
WATER WALL
59°F

SECTION AUDITORIUM

59°F
ADAPTIVE ROOF ELEMENTS
BOX
BOX
54°F

SECTION HUB

LOFT
OPEN TRAFFIC SPACES
50°F

SECTION DINING

-4°F
68°F
CONF 72°F
65°F
70°F
OFFICES 72°F 65°F
50°F

94°F
91°F
78°F
68°F
74°F
outlet 60-68°F
floor surface 68°F

60°F
72°F
74°F
outlet 68°F

50°F
70°F
68°F

23°F
66°F
75°F
58°F
70°F
outlet 70°F
floor surface 75°F

BAYER AG KONZERNZENTRALE

Leverkusen, Germany
Design 1998/Completion 2002
Client: Bayer AG
Helmut Jahn/Werner Sobek/Matthias Schuler

This project was the result of a limited International Competition. Our project was chosen based on its innovative architectural and engineering concepts proposed.

Urbanistically, the semi-elliptical shape engages the park to the south and its pergola to the north, reinforces the linearity of the adjacent street and 'confronts' the original headquarters across the street.

In order to maximize the natural resources and minimize technical equipment, we opted for a twin-shell façade. The fully glazed outer and inner glass shells enable natural ventilation, protect from noise, rain and wind and allow for placement of shades behind the outer shells. For conditioning, air is taken from the controlled airspace between the shells through the windows or a special detail at the slab edge and heated or cooled by a convector in the raised floor and distributed from there along the displacement principle. This system supports the basic heating and cooling through an integrated piping system in the coffered exposed concrete slabs.

The roof is covered in the cellular panel-system developed at the IIT Campus Center project. It acts as roofing insulation, acoustic barrier, accommodates local ventilation and admits daylight, where desired. Above the entry hall glass cells were used with particular fritting to control the solar gains.

The whole building envelope is here implemented as a highly technically controllable and adaptable skin, mediating between the exterior and the desired interior conditions, using minimal energy with maximal comfort. Bayer comes

a large step towards the goal of a building envelope approximating the wonderful adaptive capacity of the human skin.

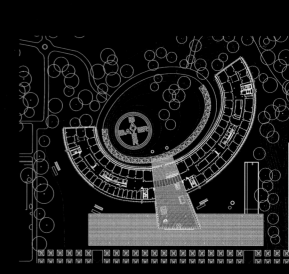

Süd

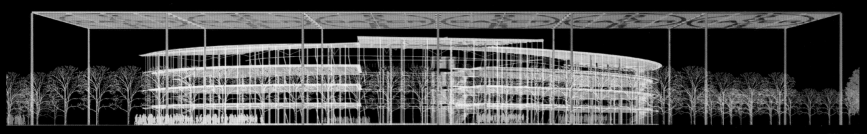

Nord

Ost

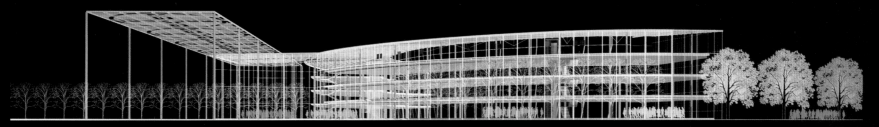

West

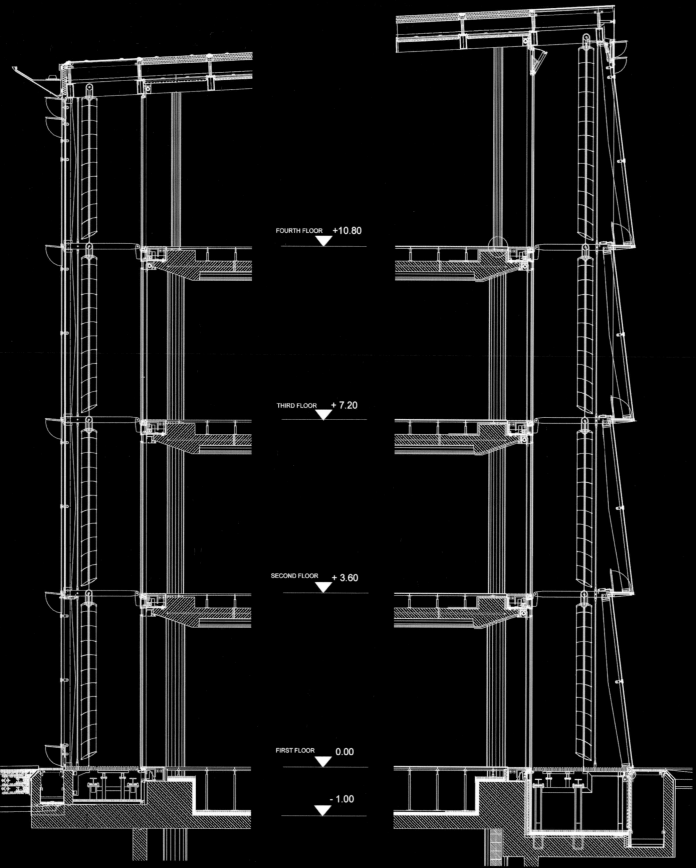

FOURTH FLOOR   +10.80

THIRD FLOOR   + 7.20

SECOND FLOOR   + 3.60

FIRST FLOOR   0.00

- 1.00

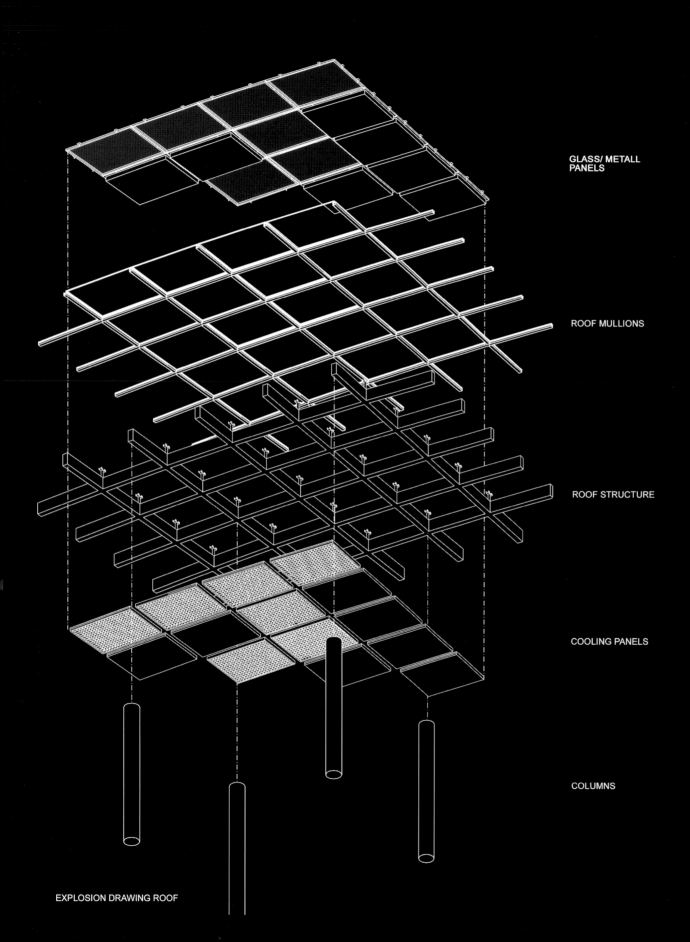

GLASS/ METALL
PANELS

ROOF MULLIONS

ROOF STRUCTURE

COOLING PANELS

COLUMNS

EXPLOSION DRAWING ROOF

MANNHEIMER 2

Mannheim, Germany
Design 2000/Completion 2004
Client: Mannheimer Holding AG
Helmut Jahn/Werner Sobek/Matthias Schuler

In 1987 we designed the new corporate head-quarters for Mannheimer Holding AG. In 2000, the need for additional space and the possible acquisition of the remainder of the city-block led to the design of the addition. The existing and new are of contrasting strategies: curved versus edgy, solid stone versus transparent glass, formal verses technical, sealed and conditioned versus open to light and air, maximizing the natural resources. The addition asserts its presence by cantilevering over part of the existing and thus connects without touching. Hans Schreiber, its Chairman, supported us all along to implement these goals. The building is now under construction.

The technical systems are, like at Bayer, based on a decentralized air system supported by integral heating and cooling in the concrete slabs. The twin-shell façade is derived from the principle of the casement window. The operable window accommodates direct air flow from the outside to the interior and seals off the over-heated air in between the outer and inner shells. Due to the reduced cooling-load, ground water use eliminates the need for cooling towers.

The curved cantilevering roof is clad with cells of stainless steel and glass along the principles developed for Bayer.

Mannheimer 2 is an example how systems and components can be applied and refined on for-mally very different structures and lead to a very different appearance, within a continuity of approach.

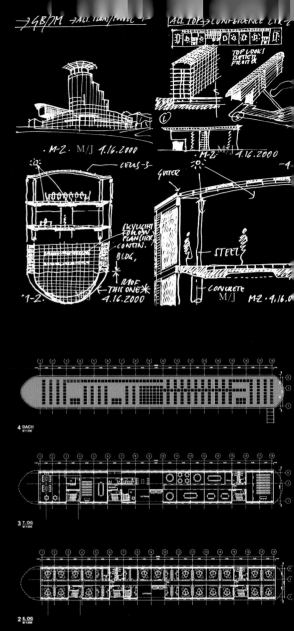

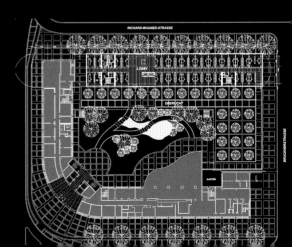

Façade system

FOCUS MEDIA ROSTOCK

Rostock, Germany
Design 2001/Completion 2004
Client: Harald Lochotzke Projekt-
entwicklung GmbH
Helmut Jahn/Werner Sobek/Matthias Schuler

Harald Lochotzke is a mover and shaker in Rostock. He came to Berlin and then to Chicago
and convinced me that I should do these three
buildings with a total area of 55.000 m², which
is very large and bold for the local market.
What intrigued me most was his innovative
concept of project delivery by controlling development, construction and leasing. The architect
and the engineers become part and share tasks
with his team, eliminating thus the confronta-
tional situations, which develop in the typical
building delivery process.

The three buildings form a new city areal in con-
tinuation of the central district. Their block-like
configuration reinforces the streets and create
urban markers at the corners and their edges.
The central building is covered by a fabric roof
with an open public space. This building houses
the DEUTSCHE MED, an equally innovative
concept of a physicians and medical building,
centralizing preventive care and research within
close proximity to Berlin and Hamburg and
offering the amenities of the nearby coast of
the Baltic Sea.

Together we developed an innovative set of
components. The structure is a composite
steel-system with pre-cast planks with spans
up to 14 m. The unitized façade is fully glazed
on internal stainless steel frames and will be
built in a special project-plant. The decentralized
heating and cooling system developed on previous projects as a perfect fit, due to an efficient envelope. The membrane roof, the screen
walls and the roof-grating are all engineered
simply and bought effectively to assure the
architectural intent at surprisingly low cost.

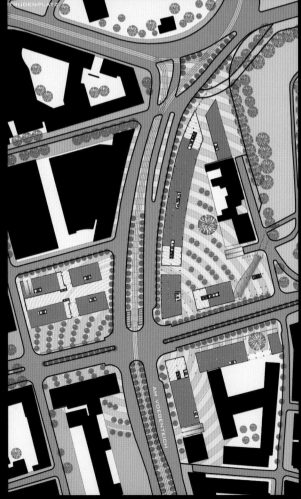

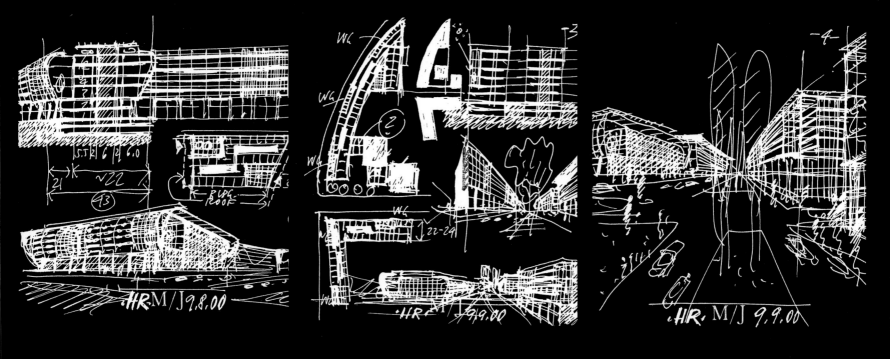

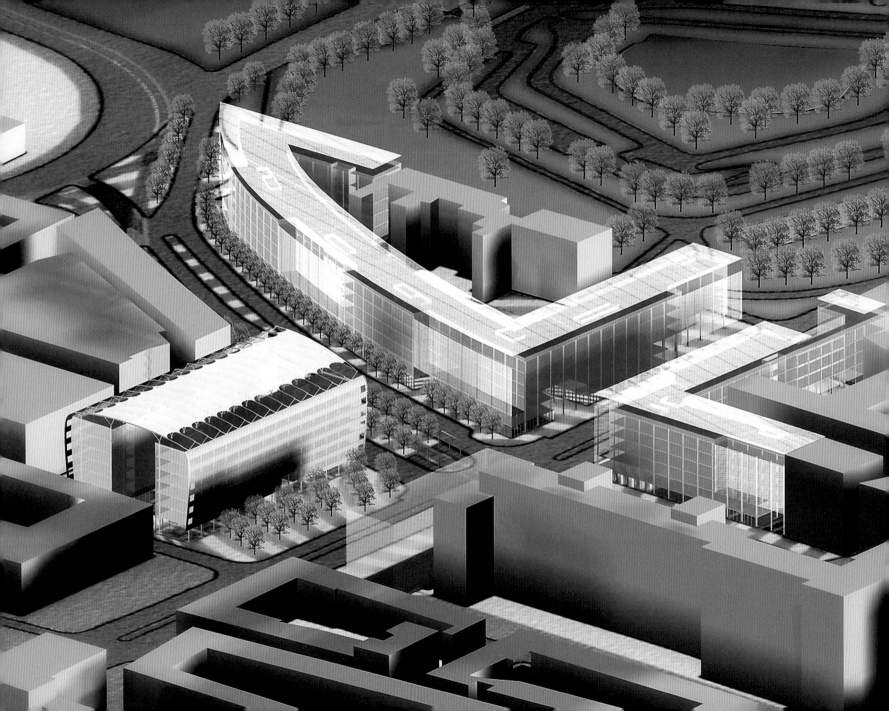

ZIRKUSWEG HAMBURG

Hamburg, Germany
Design 2001
Client: B & L Immobilien AG
Helmut Jahn/Werner Sobek/Matthias Schuler

We were commissioned for a study for an office building at a place where the edge of the central city intersects with the Reeperbahn, Hamburg's amusement district. This is presently not considered a prime office location and the building should therefore through its design establish the identity of a place.

The open triangle brings the adjacent park into the project. A louvered screen protects the Western façade and rolls over the top to form a shade-roof.

Though favorably received by city planning, the project was ultimately dropped by the client in favor of a less demanding scheme.

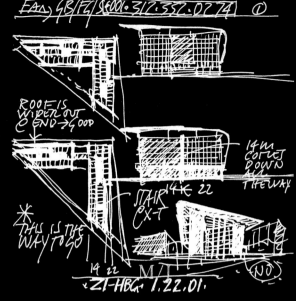

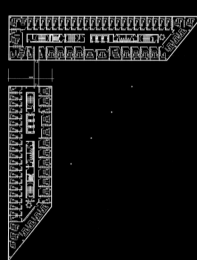

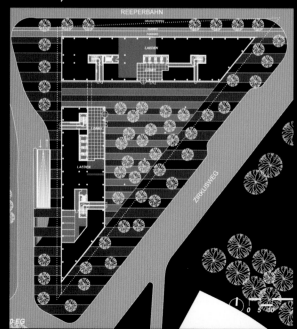

FORUM AN DER MUSEUMSINSEL

Berlin, Germany
Design 2001
Client: Freiberger Immobilien
Entwicklungs GmbH
Helmut Jahn/Werner Sobek/Matthias Schuler

This successful competition project completes the existing, landmarked historical fabric on a large block in the center of Berlin. Like a meander, weaving itself through the block, creates urban edges toward the exterior streets and spaces at the block's interiors.

Architecturally, we contrast the existing. Glass versus stone, transparency versus solid, the curved versus the gabled roof, integral versus conventional systems, linked versus closed spaces, are the result of this approach. Thus, the new building becomes a counterpoint to the existing.

The project awaits resolution of issues with City and Landmarks regarding the mix of uses and preservation of the existing.

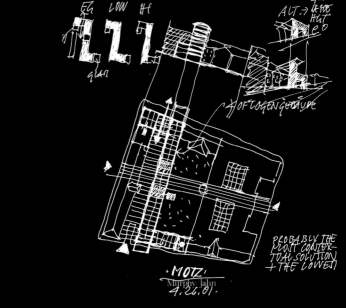

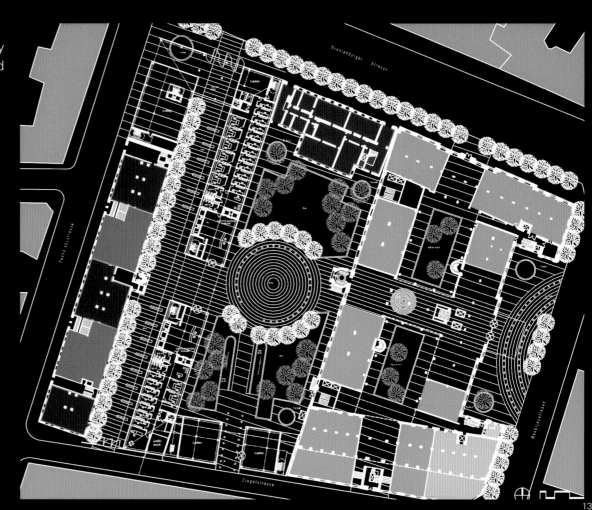

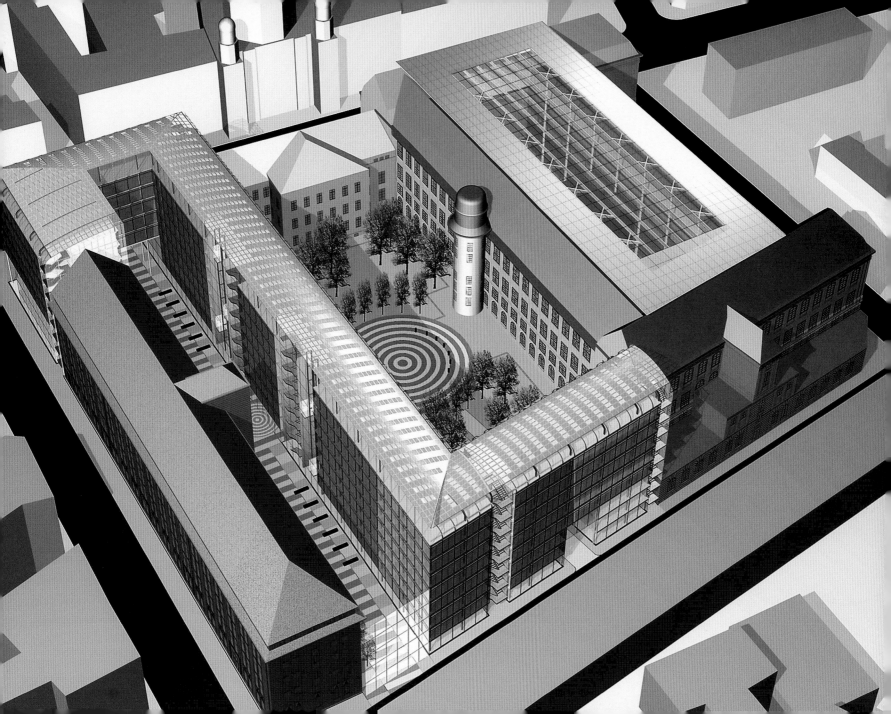

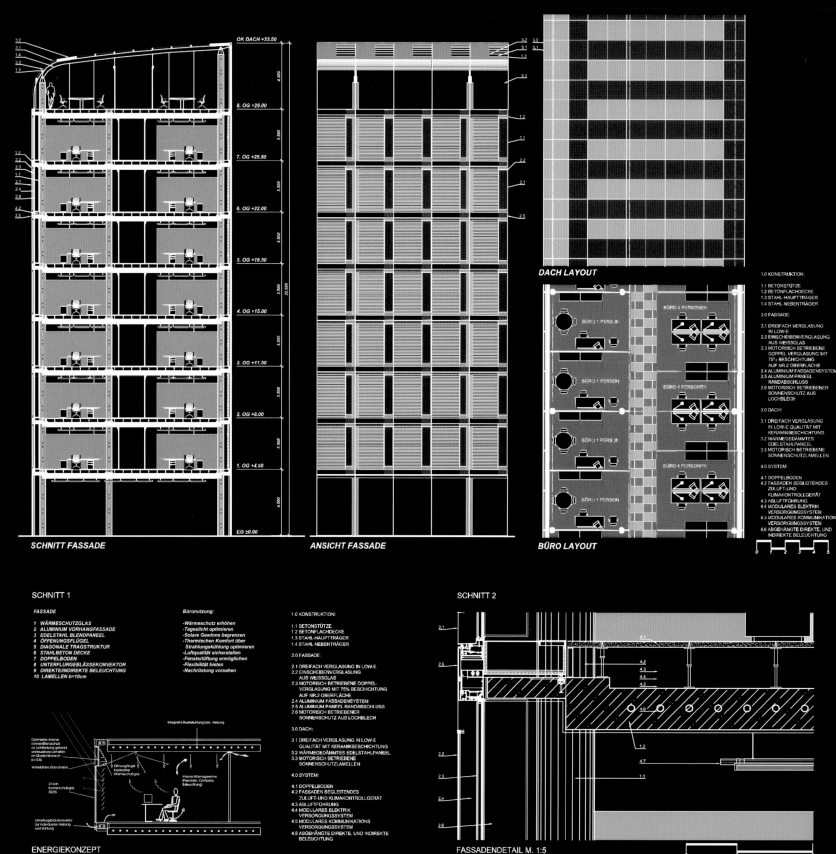

SCHNITT FASSADE

OK DACH +33.50

8. OG +29.00
7. OG +25.50
6. OG +22.00
5. OG +18.50
4. OG +15.00
3. OG +11.50
2. OG +8.00
1. OG +4.50

EG ±0.00

ANSICHT FASSADE

DACH LAYOUT

BÜRO LAYOUT

BÜRO 1 PERSON
BÜRO 4 PERSONEN

1.0 KONSTRUKTION:

1.1 BETONSTÜTZE
1.2 BETONFLACHDECKE
1.3 STAHL-HAUPTTRÄGER
1.4 STAHL-NEBENTRÄGER

2.0 FASSADE:

2.1 DREIFACH VERGLASUNG
    IN LOW-E
2.2 EINSCHEIBENVERGLASUNG
    AUS WEISSGLAS
2.3 MOTORISCH BETRIEBENE
    DOPPEL VERGLASUNG MIT
    75° BESCHICHTUNG
    AUF NR.2 OBERFLÄCHE
2.4 ALUMINIUM FASSADENSYSTEM
2.5 ALUMINIUM PANEEL
    RANDABSCHLUSS
2.6 MOTORISCH BETRIEBENER
    SONNENSCHUTZ AUS
    LOCHBLECH

3.0 DACH:

3.1 DREIFACH VERGLASUNG
    IN LOW-E QUALITÄT MIT
    KERAMIKBESCHICHTUNG
3.2 WÄRMEGEDÄMMTES
    EDELSTAHLPANEEL
3.3 MOTORISCH BETRIEBENE
    SONNENSCHUTZLAMELLEN

4.0 SYSTEM:

4.1 DOPPELBODEN
4.2 FASSADEN BEGLEITENDES
    ZULUFT-UND
    KLIMAKONTROLLGERÄT
4.3 ABLUFTFÜHRUNG
4.4 MODULARES ELEKTRIK
    VERSORGUNGSSYSTEM
4.5 MODULARES KOMMUNIKATION
    VERSORGUNGSSYSTEM
4.6 ABGEHÄNGTE DIREKTE, UND
    INDIREKTE BELEUCHTUNG

0 1 2 3 4 5

SCHNITT 1

FASSADE

1 WÄRMESCHUTZGLAS
2 ALUMINIUM VORHANGFASSADE
3 EDELSTAHL BLENDPANEEL
4 ÖFFENUNGSFLÜGEL
5 DIAGONALE TRAGSTRUKTUR
6 STAHLBETON DECKE
7 DOPPELBODEN
8 UNTERFLURGEBLÄSSEKONVEKTOR
9 DIREKTE/INDIREKTE BELEUCHTUNG
10 LAMELLEN b=10cm

Büronutzung:

-Wärmeschutz erhöhen
-Tageslicht optimieren
-Solare Gewinne begrenzen
-Thermischen Komfort über
 Strahlungskühlung optimieren
-Luftqualität sicherstellen
-Fensterlüftung ermöglichen
-Flexibilität bieten
-Nachrüstung vorsehen

1.0 KONSTRUKTION:

1.1 BETONSTÜTZE
1.2 BETONFLACHDECKE
1.3 STAHL-HAUPTTRÄGER
1.4 STAHL-NEBENTRÄGER

2.0 FASSADE:

2.1 DREIFACH VERGLASUNG IN LOW-E
2.2 EINSCHEIBENVERGLASUNG
    AUS WEISSGLAS
2.3 MOTORISCH BETRIEBENE DOPPEL-
    VERGLASUNG MIT 75% BESCHICHTUNG
    AUF NR.2 OBERFLÄCHE
2.4 ALUMINIUM FASSADENSYSTEM
2.5 ALUMINIUM PANEEL RANDABSCHLUSS
2.6 MOTORISCH BETRIEBENER
    SONNENSCHUTZ AUS LOCHBLECH

3.0 DACH:

3.1 DREIFACH VERGLASUNG IN LOW-E
    QUALITÄT MIT KERAMIKBESCHICHTUNG
3.2 WÄRMEGEDÄMMTES EDELSTAHLPANEEL
3.3 MOTORISCH BETRIEBENE
    SONNENSCHUTZLAMELLEN

4.0 SYSTEM:

4.1 DOPPELBODEN
4.2 FASSADEN BEGLEITENDES
    ZULUFT-UND KLIMAKONTROLLGERÄT
4.3 ABLUFTFÜHRUNG
4.4 MODULARES ELEKTRIK
    VERSORGUNGSSYSTEM
4.5 MODULARES KOMMUNIKATIONS
    VERSORGUNGSSYSTEM
4.6 ABGEHÄNGTE DIREKTE, UND INDIREKTE
    BELEUCHTUNG

SCHNITT 2

ENERGIEKONZEPT

FASSADENDETAIL M. 1:5

SCHNITT 1

SCHNITT 2

ILLINOIS INSTITUTE OF TECHNOLOGY
STUDENT HOUSING

Chicago, Illinois
Design 2001/Completion 2003
Client: IIT Housing Corporation
Helmut Jahn/Werner Sobek/Matthias Schuler

Through an invited competition we won the commission for the IIT-Student Housing. The site, across the college's Main Quadrangle and Mies' Crown-Hall, has to respond both to the Quadrangle as a space defining wall, as well be pervious, allowing east-west movement through the campus, which is divided through the north-south barriers of State Street and the elevated train.

Between three U-shaped buildings forming entry-courts are two 'sally-ports'. Facing the railway line glass screens protect against the noise of the trains. The curved west-façade of profiled stainless steel panels merges at the set-back-floor into the roof and reinforces the idea of an extrusion. At the courts and sally-ports the wall projects and the panels are perforated and form screened gates.

The low budget did not allow planning for long-term energy/comfort measures in the MEP-system. However, the comfort of the user has been improved by simple means, like coated, low-E glass, maximizing daylight, natural ventilation and a specially designed furniture system allowing the students maximum flexibility in placement and use.

The earlier project for the Campus Center occupied partially the same site. Its program and use led to a building of components, which are flexible, adaptable and exchangeable over the buildings' life. The housing project did not require such a strategy, but resulted in a clear response to the urban condition with a bold curved form and industrial materials facing the rigor of the Mies-Campus. This is a big task, 35 years after I arrived at the Campus to study at IIT.

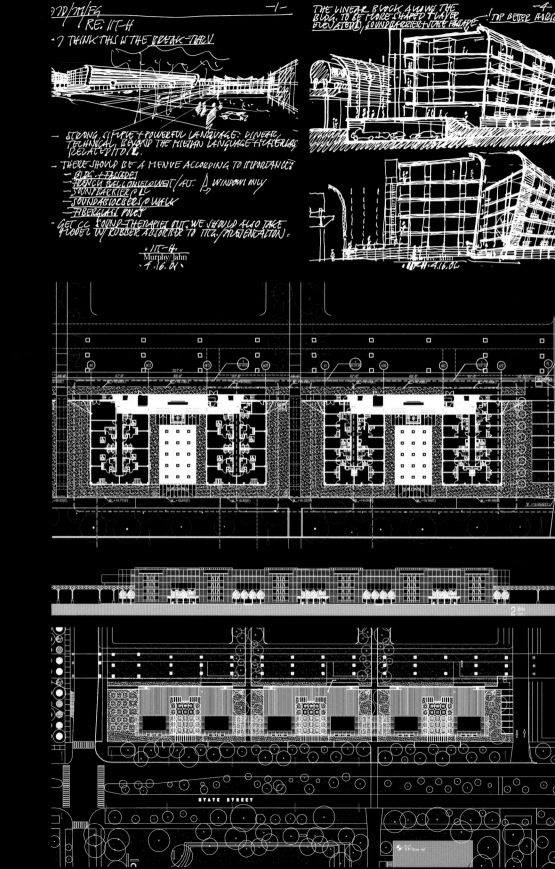

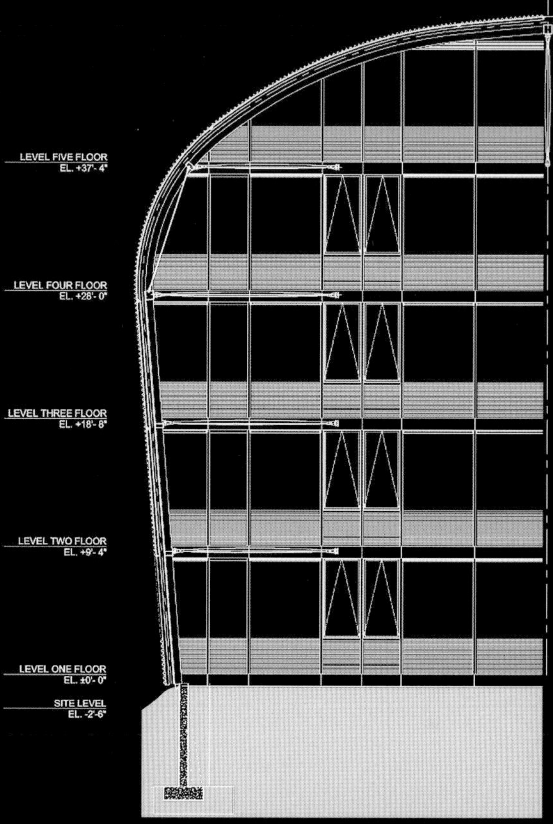

LEVEL FIVE FLOOR
EL. +37'- 4"

LEVEL FOUR FLOOR
EL. +28'- 0"

LEVEL THREE FLOOR
EL. +18'- 8"

LEVEL TWO FLOOR
EL. +9'- 4"

LEVEL ONE FLOOR
EL. ±0'- 0"

SITE LEVEL
EL. -2'-6"

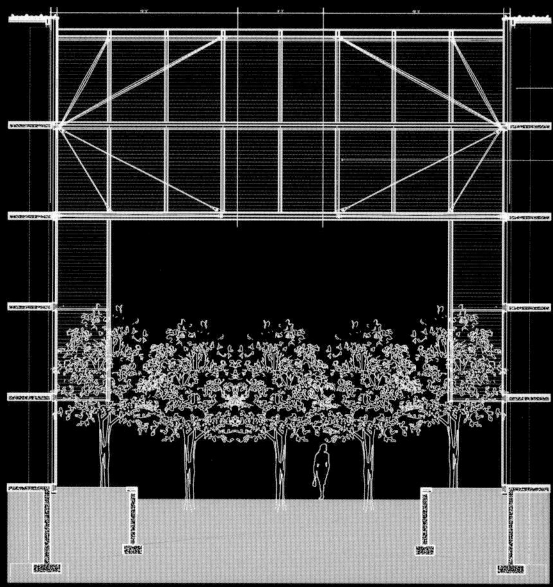

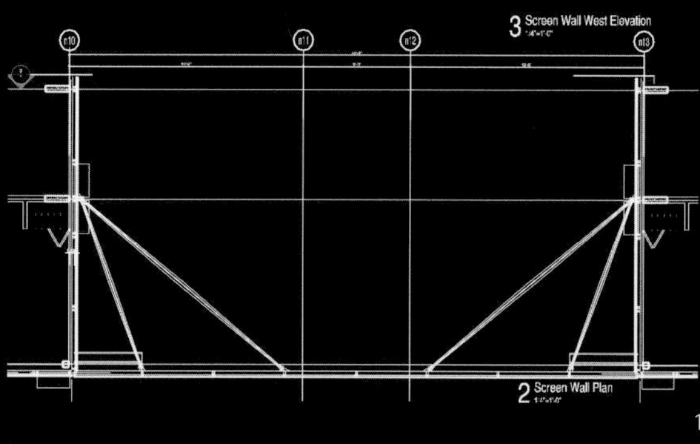

3 Screen Wall West Elevation

2 Screen Wall Plan

1 Wing Wall Section
1/4"=1'-0"

2 Wing Wall Plan
1/4"=1'-0"

UNIQUE AIRPORT ZURICH

Zurich, Switzerland
Design 2001
Client: Unique Airport City
Helmut Jahn/Werner Sobek/Matthias Schuler

This unsuccessful entry to an international competition was a further contribution to the subject 'Airport City', previously dealt with and realized at the Munich Airport.

The extensive program was challenged by a limited siting opportunity at the base of the Bützenbühl Hill, a nature preserve at the airport. The other boundary is the airport-roadway-system, which forms a horseshoe around the hill.

The idea was to create an oasis within the sprawling tarmac of the airfield. The individual building wings are arranged on an irregular, radial pattern. Their length defined by the axial length from the roadway to the edge of the hill. This assures all buildings' views of the Bützenbühl. From the air the buildings are reminiscent of airplane fuselages in the airfield. From the ground the glassy wings become pavilions in the park.

Building parts and components proposed for structure, cladding, roof and energy/comfort-system are similar to those developed on built work.

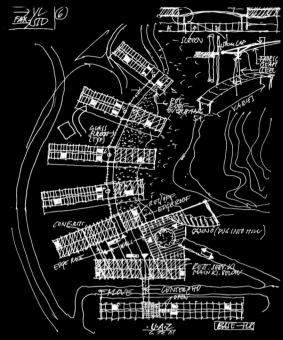

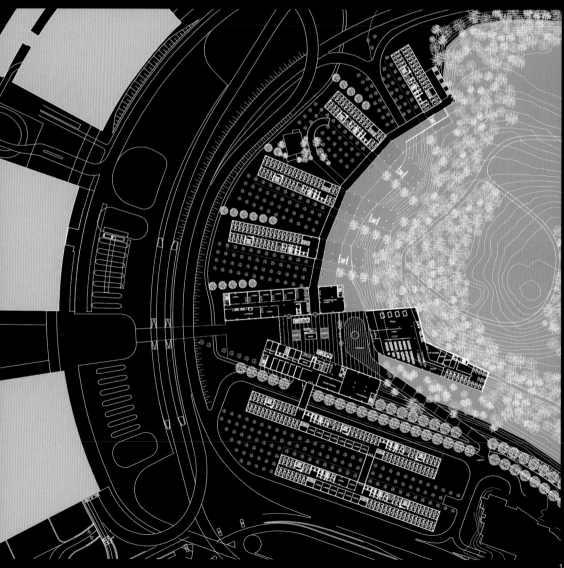

SPINATHAUS – BUDAPEST

Budapest, Hungary
Design 2001
Client: Bayerische Hausbau GmbH
Helmut Jahn/Werner Sobek/Matthias Schuler

In an invited competition we proposed to trans-
form a brutalist concrete structure of the 60's
into an open, transparent and light-filled work
environment.

A strategy was proposed to achieve a distinctly
different technical and constructional aesthetic,
contrasting the neighboring classical buildings.
The front wall is changed from the existing,
heavy concrete wall to a floor-high glass wall
with a light mesh-screen wall in front of it.
Terraces between the screen and the façade
give those offices special amenities, with views
to the Danube River and the Castle.

The proposed systems are geared towards the
buildings' existing structure along the principles
of maximizing natural resources, reducing technical equipment and optimizing comfort.

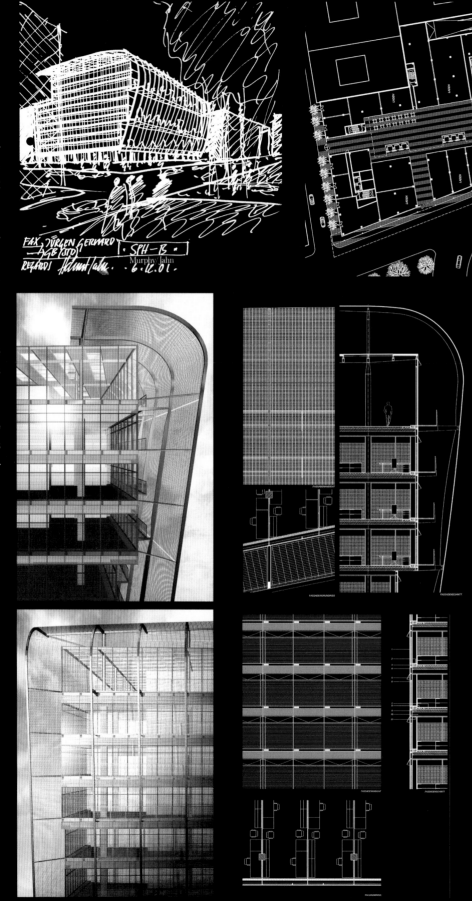

HORIZON SERONO

Geneva, Switzerland
Design 2002/Completion 2005
Client: Serono International SA
Helmut Jahn/Werner Sobek/Matthias Schuler
Associate Architect: E. Barth, P. Pellacani,
P. Freiburghaus Architects

The design is inspired by the challenge Serono has set itself to be the biggest and the best Biotech Company in the world. Serono and its people have a vision about its products and how the company interacts within and with the public.

The site is difficult and challenging and thus offers a great opportunity. Its history goes back to 1892, linked to the emergence of electricity in Geneva. At its full built out in the 50's the site had a strong, block-like character, consisting of large scale simple industrial buildings with a dense urban character.

The result is not a building, but a city-block of a series of existing and new structures with space, covered or open, flowing between them. The "Main Streets" become the central organizing elements and interchange with the public and links with the internal and more private areas of the Headquarters and the World Research Center. They lead to the 'Forum' in the heart of the complex, a meeting and entertainment space which brings the company together. Along its perimeter boundaries the building is seen never as a whole but in fragments, yet with a consistent image. This image of the screens with crystalline glass blocks behind is strong, but not intimidating, soft rather than hard, porous for view and air, creating a magical and changing boundary to the public realm.

Equally important is the landscaping. Every court is half garden and half linear plaza. Tall trees in the gardens can also be seen from the higher levels.

In terms of construction and performance the building is more informed by principles of science and technology, rather than design and style. Horizon Serono uses new energy concepts that assume responsibility for more than form and aesthetic. Daylight, natural ventilation, solar energy and the idea that a building modulates its own climate are the basic concepts to maximize the use of natural resources and minimize technical and mechanical equipment. This results in a building of high technology, but low energy consumption.

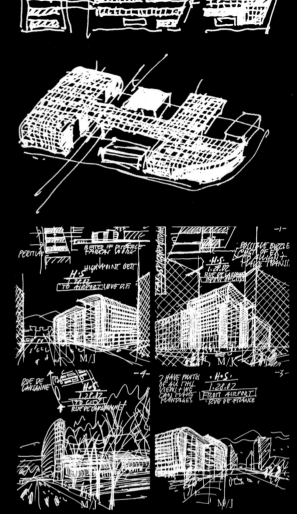

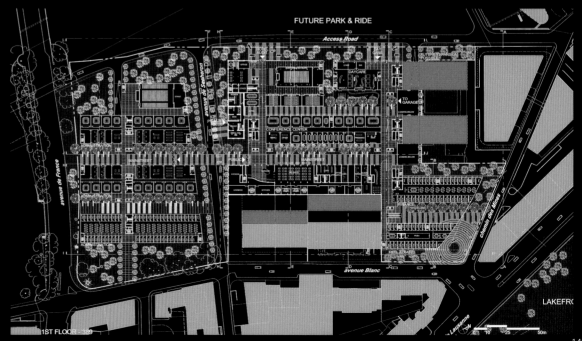

148

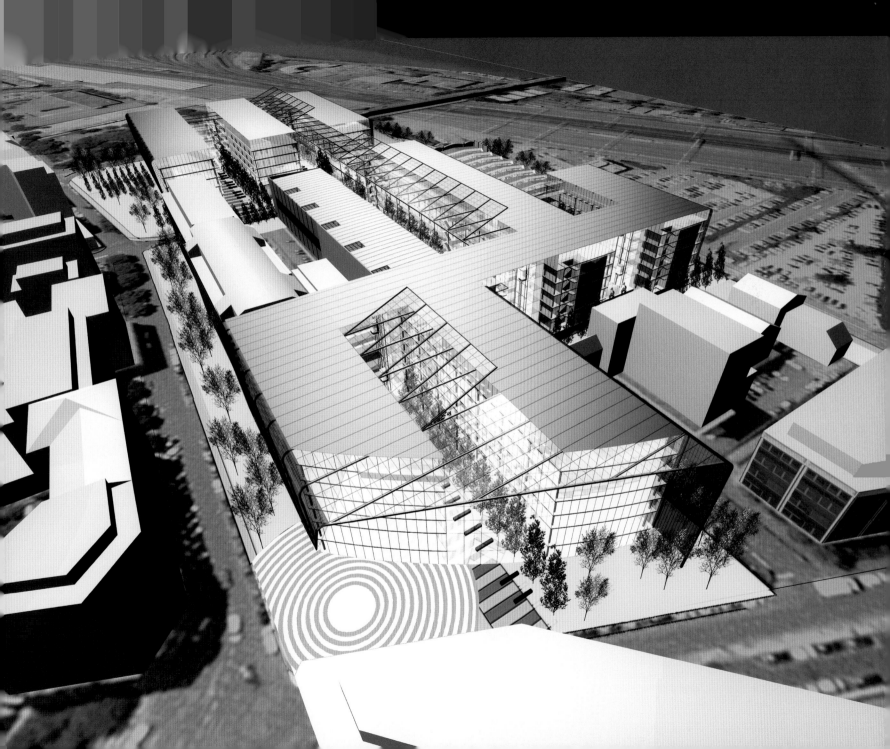

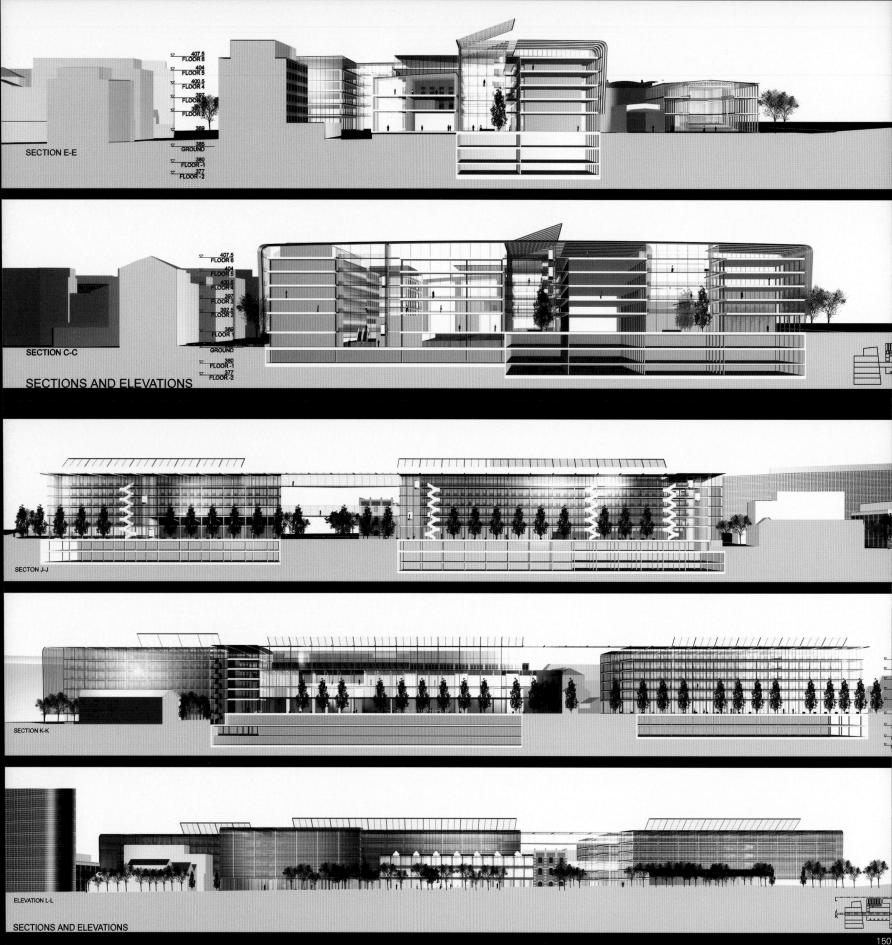

SECTION E-E

407.5
FLOOR 6
404
FLOOR 5
400.5
FLOOR 4
397
FLOOR 3
392.5
FLOOR 2
389
GROUND
385
380
FLOOR -1
377
FLOOR -2

SECTION C-C

407.5
FLOOR 6
404
FLOOR 5
400.5
FLOOR 4
397
FLOOR 3
392.5
FLOOR 2
389
FLOOR 1
GROUND
380
FLOOR -1
377
FLOOR -2

SECTIONS AND ELEVATIONS

SECTON J-J

SECTON J-J

SECTION K-K

ELEVATION L-L

SECTIONS AND ELEVATIONS

GROSSES ZIRKUSDREIECK

Hamburg, St. Pauli, Germany
Design 2002
Client: Quantum Immobilien AG
Wilhelm Bartels Bavaria-
Beteiligungs GmbH & Co KG
Helmut Jahn/Werner Sobek/Matthias Schuler

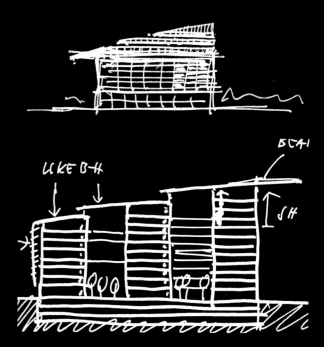

The design which was prepared for an invited competition is simple and clear and consists of three office buildings set in a spacious park. The buildings are different in footprint and height. Following the triangle shape of the site the footprints are getting smaller to the north, as their height increases.

Along the new Zirkusweg the buildings are slightly curved, opening up the space to a plaza next to the "Astra" highrise. The open spaces between the buildings, half garden, half walkway, connect the park to the east with the proposed development to the west of the Zirkusweg.

The glass roofs covering the passages create, in connection with the screens to the north and south, a large-scale building, taking relation to the smaller scale of the surrounding buildings thanks to it's clearly defined elements and structured design.

In the "skyline" above the harbor the building makes a prominent statement without competing with the "Astra" highrise. It is horizontal layered, is open and airy, almost like a sail above the existing buildings.

The full glass façade creates crystalline buildings with unobstructed views in both directions. Small balconies behind the screens further enhance the relationship to the inner city. The elevators are located between the buildings serving the connecting bridges.

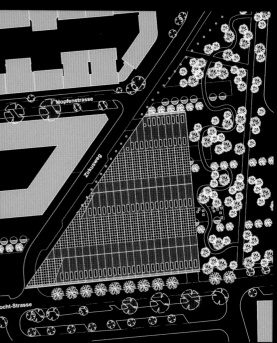

Ansicht Nord

Ansicht Süd

Ansicht Ost

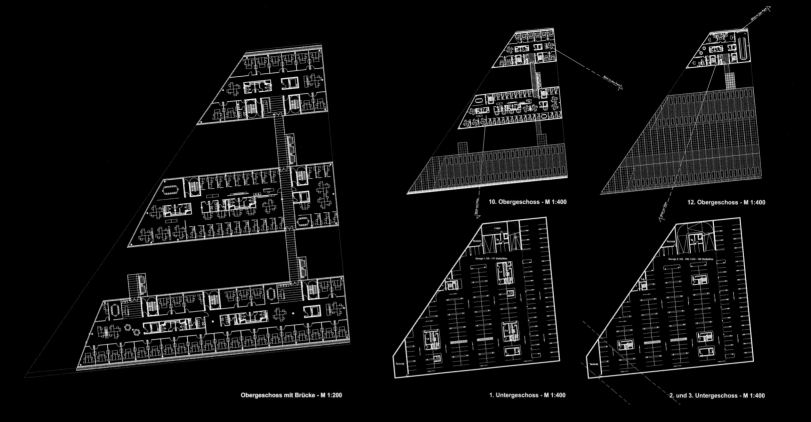

Obergeschoss mit Brücke - M 1:200

10. Obergeschoss - M 1:400

12. Obergeschoss - M 1:400

1. Untergeschoss - M 1:400

2. und 3. Untergeschoss - M 1:400

COLUMBUS CIRCLE

New York, New York
Competition 1997
Client: TishmanSpeyer Properties
Helmut Jahn/Werner Sobek

In 1997, we participated with TishmanSpeyer Properties in a developer competition to replace the New York Coliseum on Columbus Circle with a commercial project.

This project was the first of a series of towers worldwide, which transferred the principles of integral engineering and technology developed on the lower buildings.

At Columbus Circle, the goal also was to explore the expressive potential of glass with simple geometric shapes. The screens at the base, the corners and the top, reinforce or blur the reading of these parts. Transparency, translucency or reflectivity and alternating different conditions of weather and time make a simple and beautiful statement.

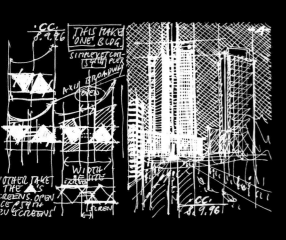

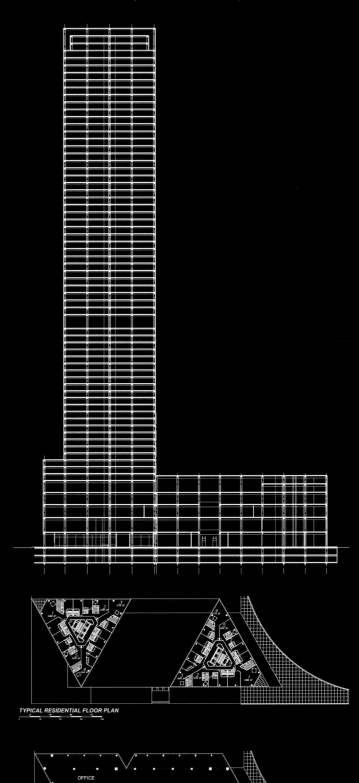

TYPICAL RESIDENTIAL FLOOR PLAN

TYPICAL OFFICE FLOOR PLAN

ZENTRALE DEUTSCHE POST

Bonn, Germany
Design 1997/Completion 2002
Client: Deutsche Post AG
Helmut Jahn/Werner Sobek/Matthias Schuler
Associate Architect: Heinle, Wischer und
Partner

In 1997, Werner Sobek and I discussed our design for the competition for the Deutsche Post over dinner. It was Werner who suggested that the shape be soft and aerodynamic mediating at its location between the City and the Rhine Park. That night, the concept of the split and shifted half-shells emerged and it withstood three rounds of the competition proceedings and nine months later, we were commissioned. It was through Managing Director, Dieter Petram's support and patronage that the post-tower, completed by the end of 2002, will be our most defining high-rise to-date. It becomes the new corporate statement for the privatized former government-owned company now Deutsche Post World Net, a statement of a progressive corporate policy.

The twin-shell façade is shingled at the south and straight at the north to facilitate the required airflow to the operable windows or decentralized perimeter convectors, which heat and cool the spaces with a displacement system. Return air is drawn through the corridors and used to condition the Skygardens. Integrated heating and cooling in the concrete structure accomplishes the basic conditioning. All those systems use water as the most efficient low-Energy carrier. Cooling is through Rhine water. A computerized building management system controls all these components and the shades within the twin shell. The most effective operational mode is found, balancing the exterior and the desired interior conditions for optimal user comfort. At night, the building's office lighting will interplay with computer controlled light-art by Yann Kersalé, making the half shells glow in selected changing colors.

This building comes closest, for a high-rise, of using minimal technical equipment while maximizing natural resources. All the parts support each other and determine the design. Nothing must be added and nothing can be taken away.

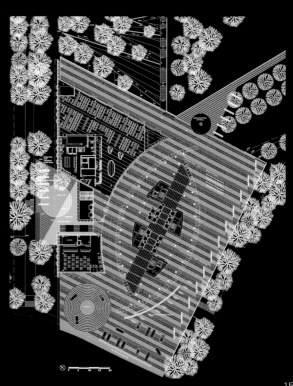

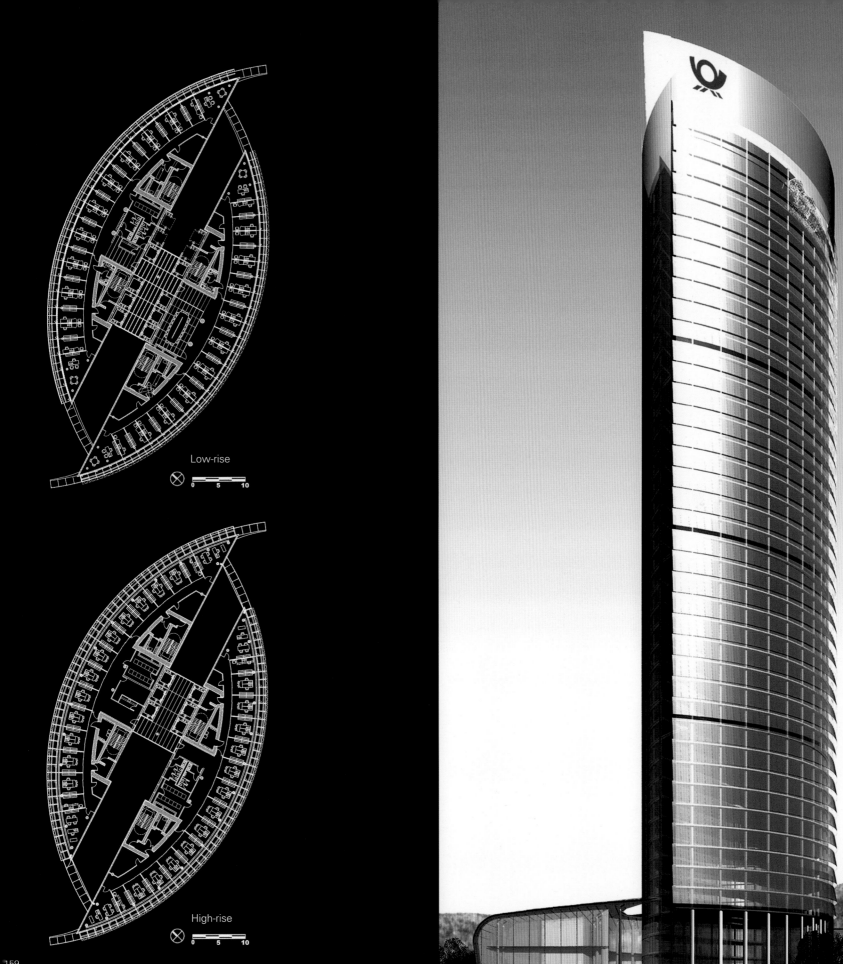

Low-rise

⊗ 0 5 10

High-rise

⊗ 0 5 10

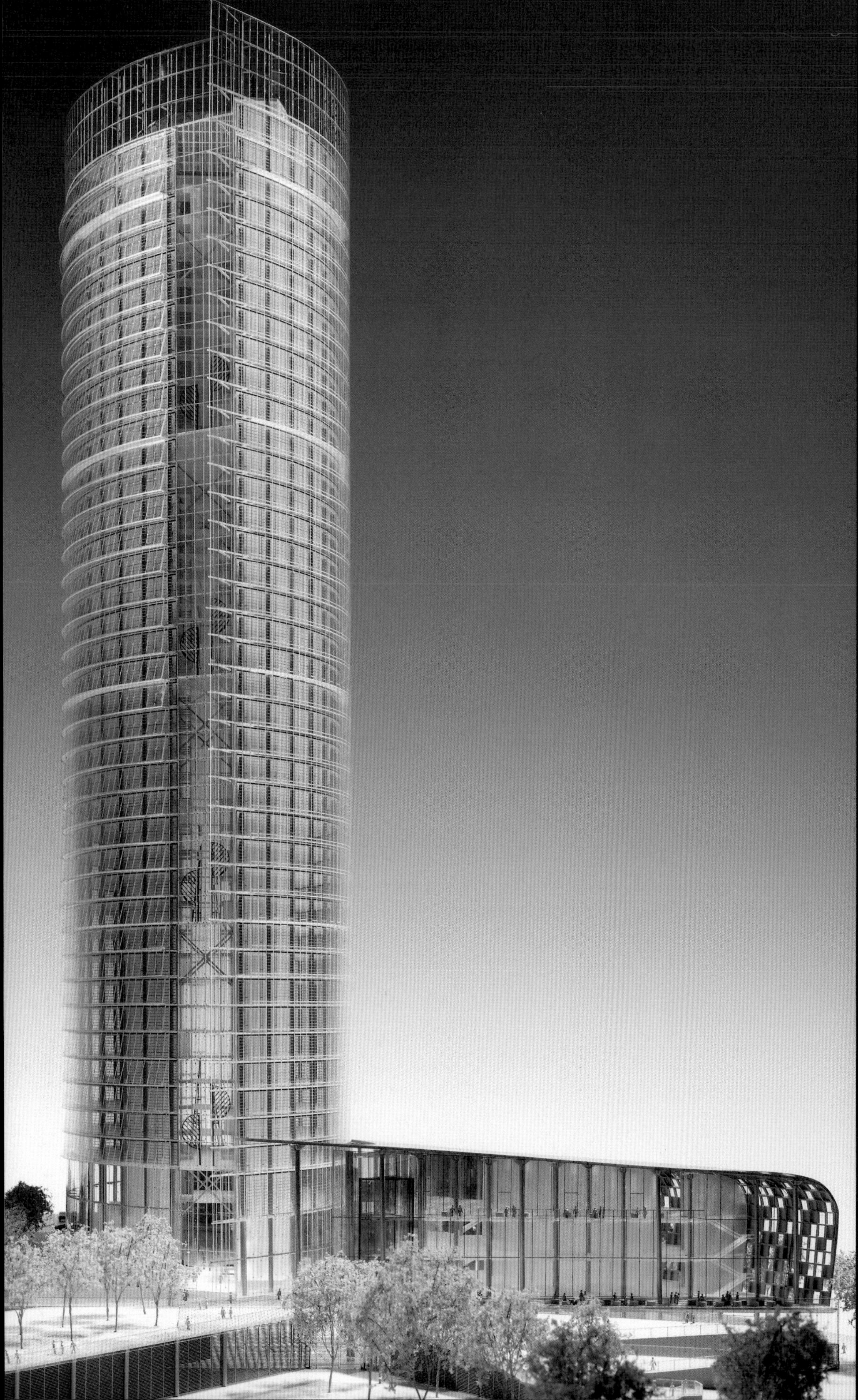

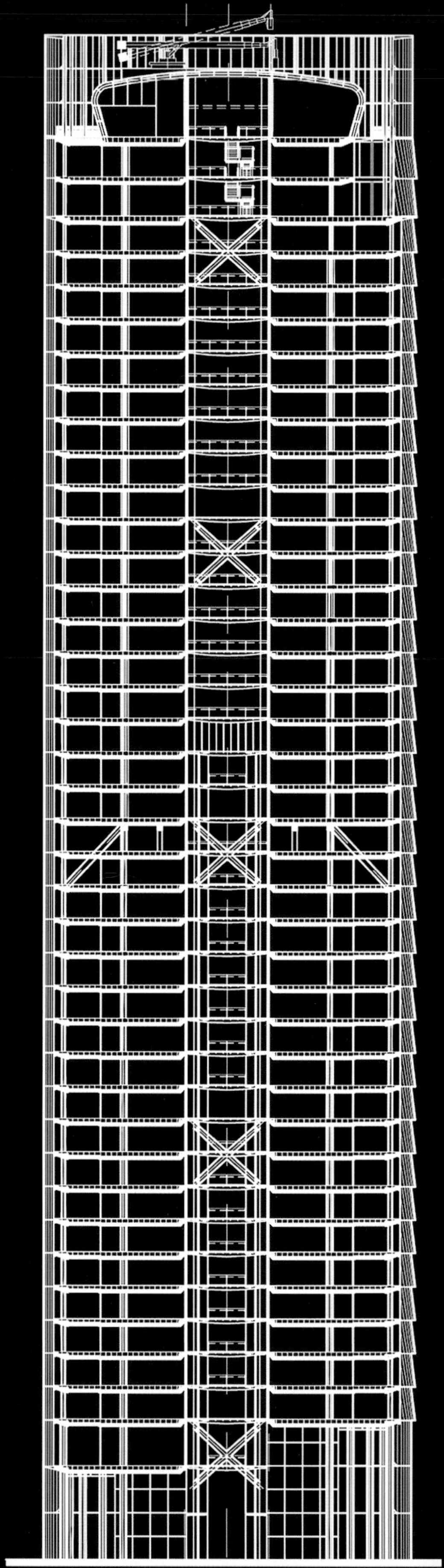

QUERSCHNITT

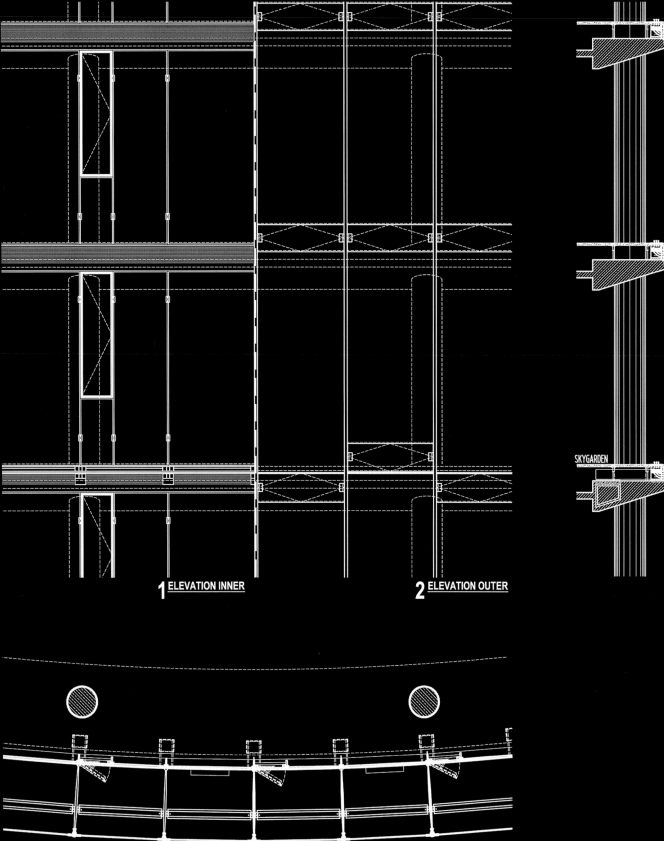

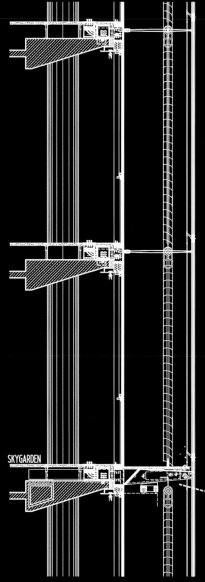

1 ELEVATION INNER

2 ELEVATION OUTER

3 SECTION

SKYGARDEN

4 PLAN

North façade

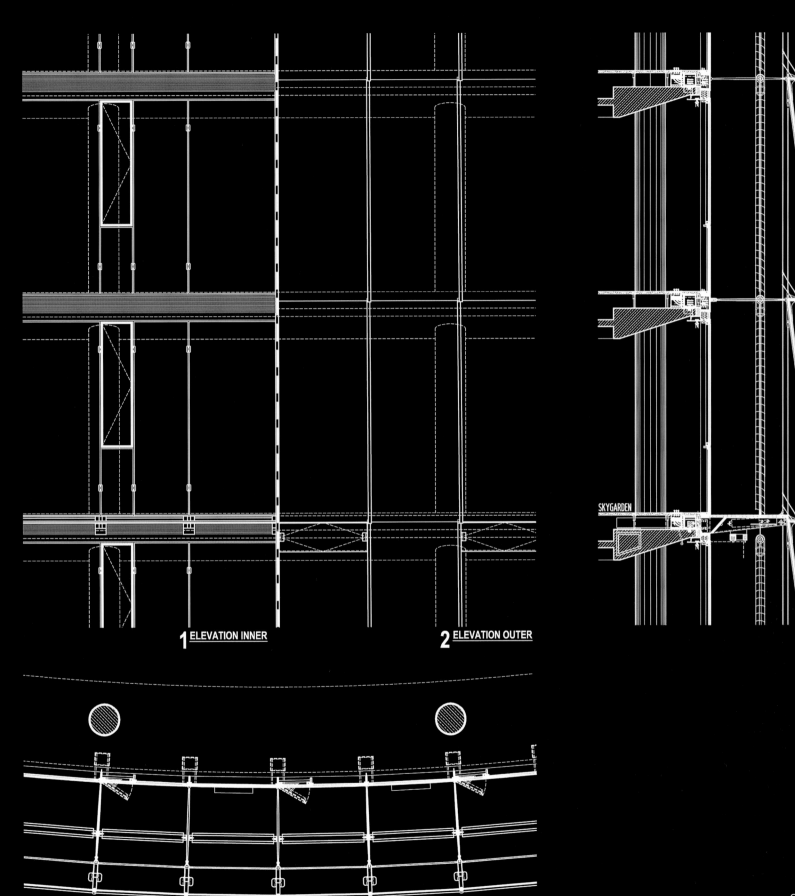

1 ELEVATION INNER 2 ELEVATION OUTER 3 SECTION

SKYGARDEN

South façade

MAX

Frankfurt, Germany
Design 2000
Client: Deutsche Grundbesitz
Management GmbH
Helmut Jahn/Werner Sobek/Matthias Schuler
Associate Architect: Köhler Architekten BDA

This commission came from a competition in the year 2000. The shape resulted from its central location in Frankfurt's high-rise bulk, softly weaving through the block and responding to its various high neighbors.

The other task and goal was to find a technical strategy to implement in a commercial building energy-savings and comfort measures, like at the Deutsche Post, with still less effort and cost.

This resulted in the development of a new type of façade. The 1.4 m module is divided into narrow double glazed, operable windows behind vertical perforated panels of stainless steel and fixed, triple glazing. Its exterior sheet is heat absorbing and reduces solar transmission by 62 %, yet allows for 75 % of daylight to pass through. The interior shade reduces energy-transmission by another 50 %. This results in the room comfort being primarily affected by interior loads. The perforated stainless steel panels in front of the operable windows serve as sun, wind, rain, acoustic and safety protection. They allow that in a 60-story high-rise the windows being opened at the top. From the inside they give an interesting modulation to the views, from the outside they reinforce the de-sired verticality.

Results of further testing in the wind tunnel and the factory also allowed us to use the decentralized convector-system with displacement distribution and non-ducted return air in a single shell façade. Since the amount of air is reduced to two air changes/hour through the buildings basic integrated heating and cooling system. The return airshafts are reduced and no supply

air-shafts are needed with the decentralized system. The building has no ducts and no suspended ceilings and higher room heights. Flexibility, efficiency and individual control are optimized in a commercial high-rise.

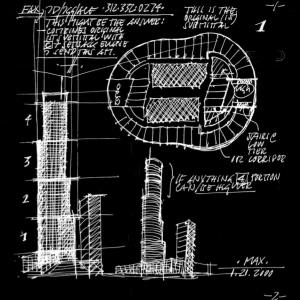

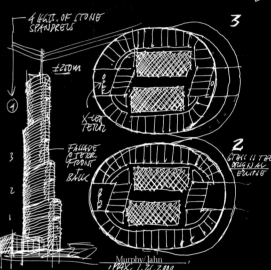

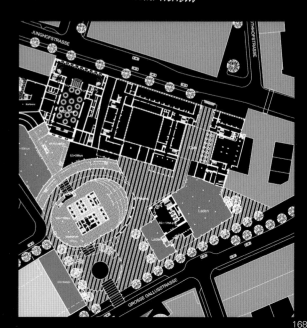

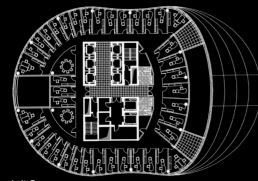

Abschnitt 7

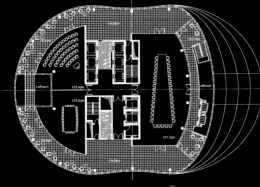

Vorstand / Konferenz

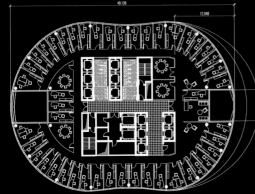

Abschnitt 3

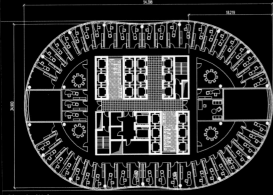

Abschnitt 1

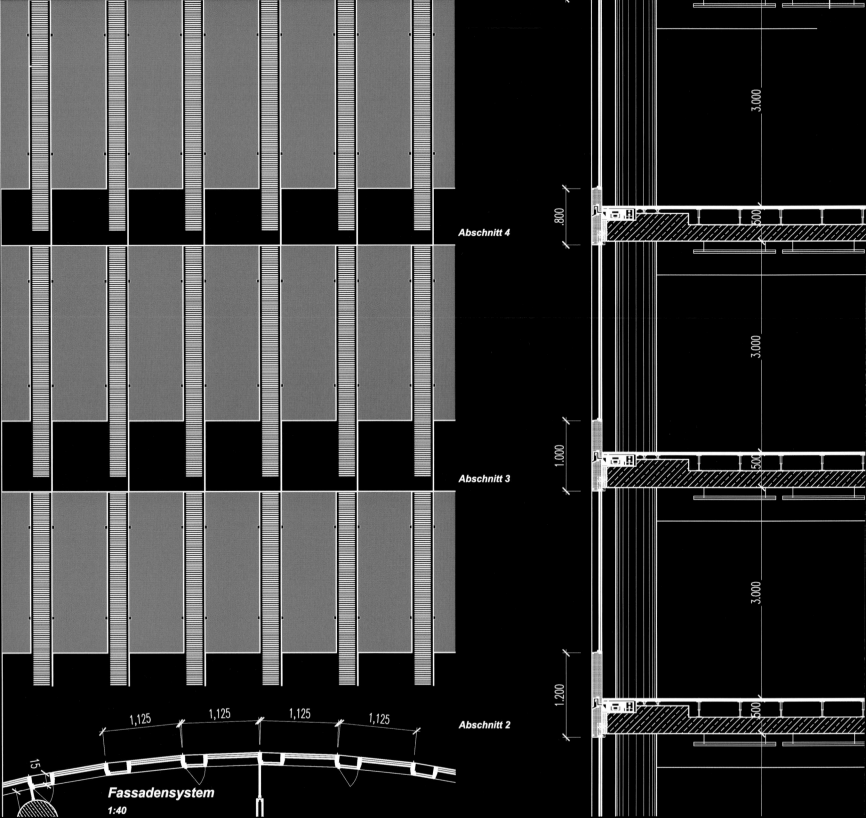

Abschnitt 4

Abschnitt 3

Abschnitt 2

.800

1.000

1.200

3.000

3.000

3.000

500

500

500

1,125   1,125   1,125   1,125

15

Fassadensystem
1:40

BISHOPSGATE

London, England
Design 2001
Client: DIFA
Helmut Jahn/Werner Sobek/Matthias Schuler

London's central financial district is undergoing a dramatic change. Norman Foster's Swiss Re Tower has been approved and is under construction. Other towers submitted awaiting approval or projects are prepared for submittal. DIFA has commissioned us to prepare an application for Bishopsgate.

The circular shape allows for the largest and most efficient footprint at the tight irregular site. A spiral linear helps to orient the building to the street and to the skyline culminating at top with an operable roof. The office-functions are interspersed with public functions like thruway and shops at grade, wellness centers, restaurants and cafes at the skylobby and at the top, television studios with an observation deck and roof garden. The all glass façade is shingled and allows at the slab edges for natural ventilation and air intake for the convectors, which condition the perimeter zone. The interior is conditioned by a central displacement system in the raised floor, both assisted by a cooled suspended ceiling. This combination of systems results from the increased lease-span of this tower, compared to the German buildings.

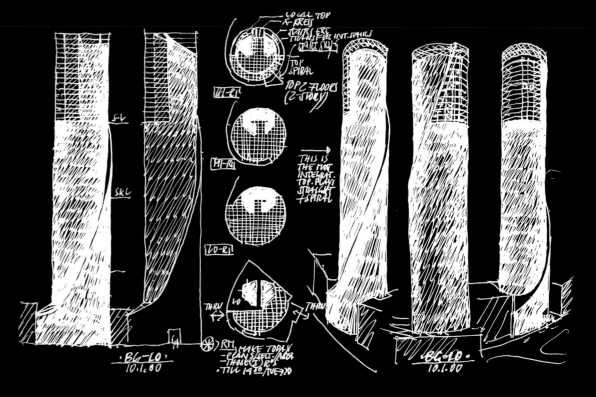

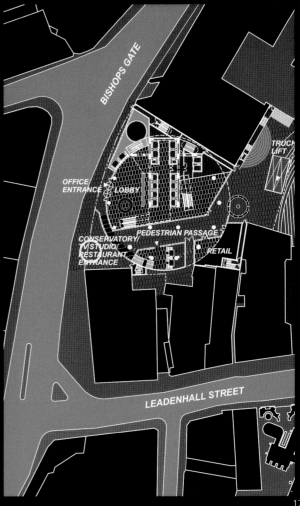

KY LOBBY PLAN

IGH RISE PLAN

OW MIDRISE PLAN

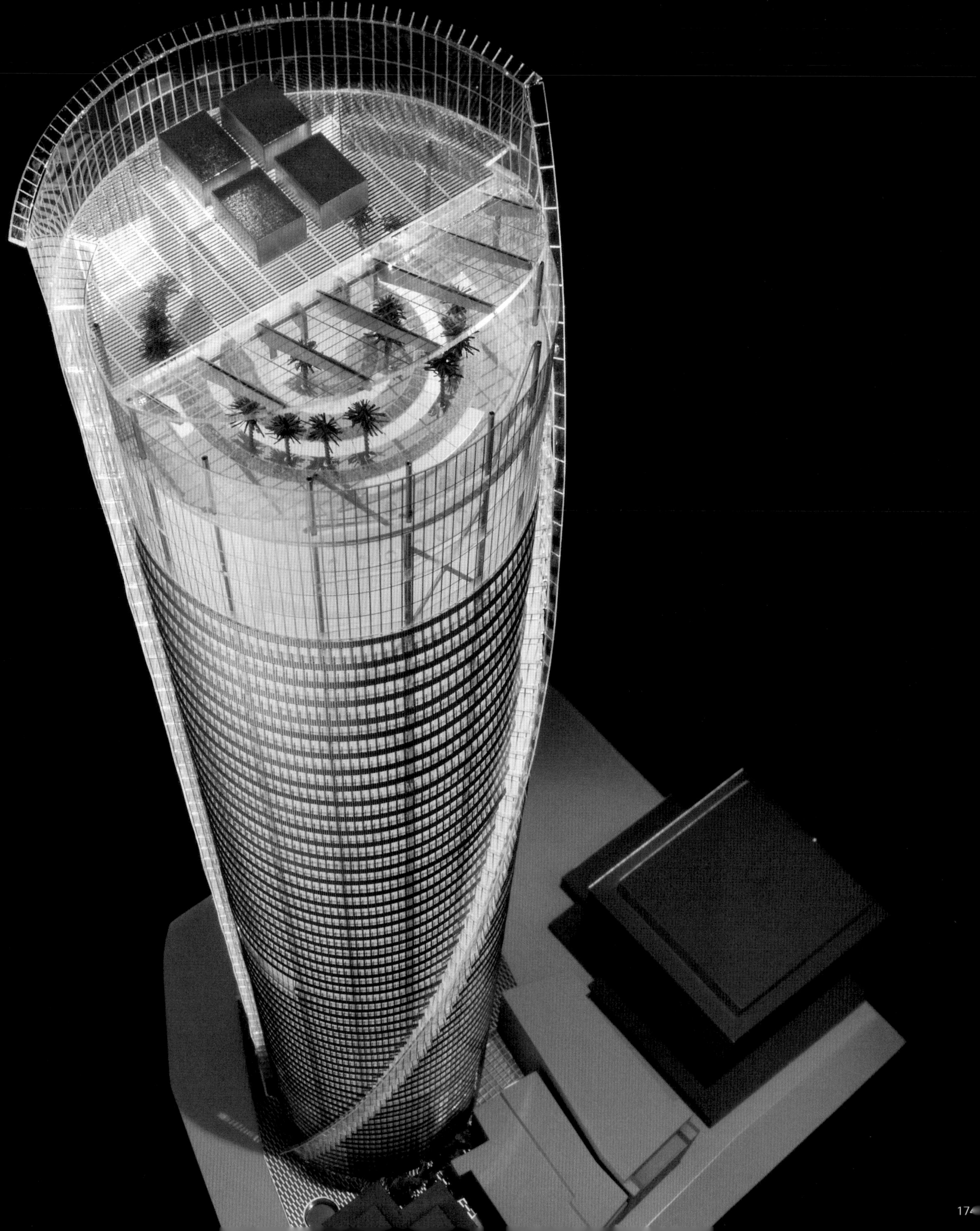

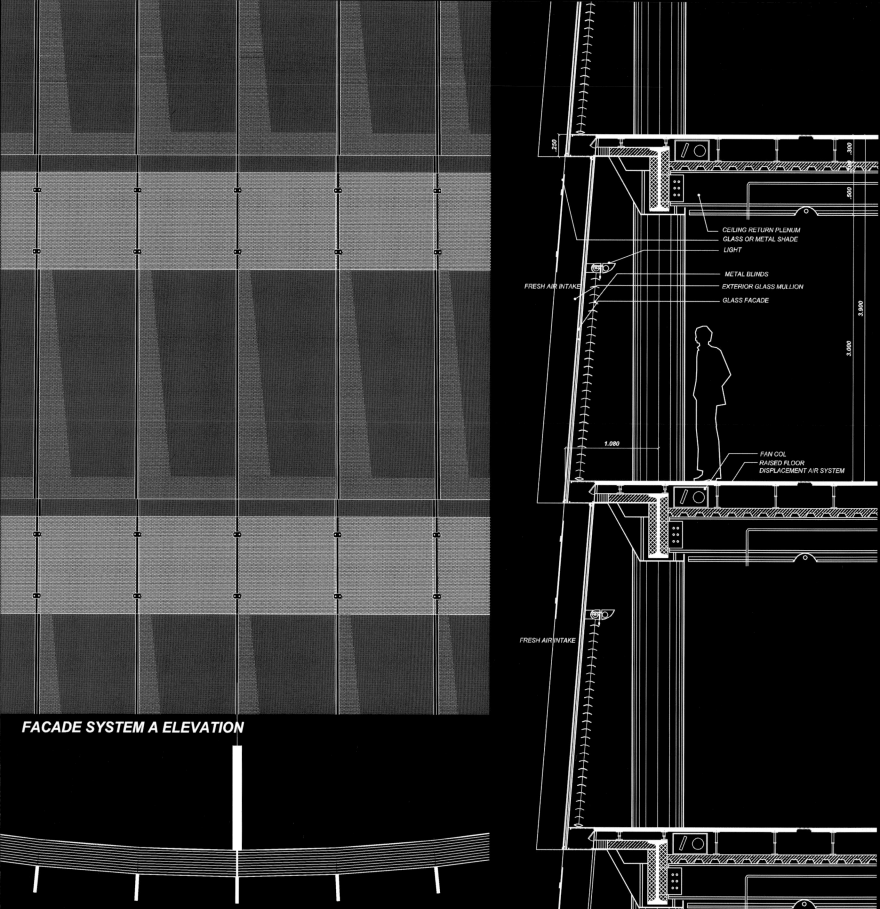

FACADE SYSTEM A ELEVATION

CEILING RETURN PLENUM
GLASS OR METAL SHADE
LIGHT

METAL BLINDS
EXTERIOR GLASS MULLION

FRESH AIR INTAKE

GLASS FACADE

FAN COL
RAISED FLOOR
DISPLACEMENT AIR SYSTEM

FRESH AIR INTAKE

1.080

.250

.300

.500

3.900

3.000

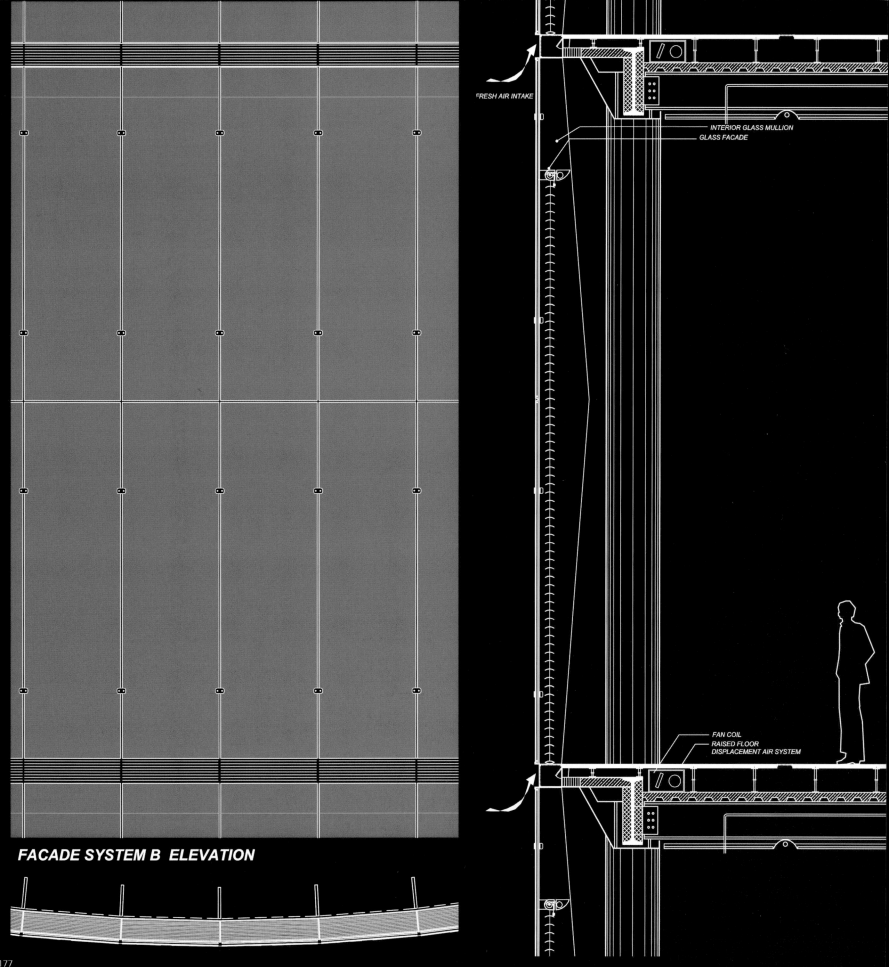

FACADE SYSTEM B ELEVATION

FRESH AIR INTAKE

INTERIOR GLASS MULLION
GLASS FACADE

FAN COIL
RAISED FLOOR
DISPLACEMENT AIR SYSTEM

HOCHHAUSENSEMBLE AM MUNCHNER TOR

Munich, Germany
Design 2001/Completion 2004
Client: Köllmann AG
Helmut Jahn/Werner Sobek/Matthias Schuler

The project was the result of an invited competition. It is part of an entirely new district of Munich, the Parkstadt Schwabing. Around a central park building blocks for office and residential uses have been established in the Masterplan. On the eastern edge of the park, along the autobahn, the urban plan calls for 5–7-story buildings, framed by towers at the southern and northern ends.

The high-rise complex forms a distinct urban sign at the south. To the north and west two low buildings form a smooth transition to the height of the adjacent building blocks.

The two slender slabs with connecting bridges read like one tower, reinforced through their overall parallelogram plan configuration and sloped roof-scape.

The towers are stiffened independently through a diagonal steel-bracing system, which acts with the composite columns and concrete slabs.

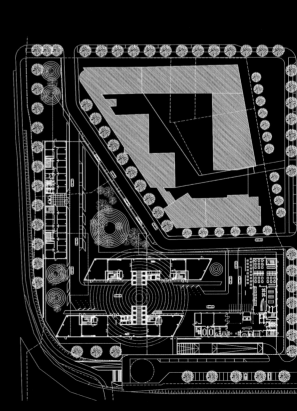

The façade is based on the principles developed for MAX: fixed triple glazing with operable double glazed windows, shaded by perforated stainless steel panels. The high thermal quality of the envelope allows reduced technical equipment and increased comfort. Basic conditioning is provided by an integrated heating and cooling system activating the mass of the concrete structure. The client did not opt for the decentralized air-system, but chose a more conservative displacement system, supplied by two fan-rooms/floor taking fresh air through the façade. This is a way combining the advantages of a decentralized system with a central air-supply. The minimal technical- and shaft-space needed assures a building with maximum flexibility, efficiency and comfort.

Ventilated façade

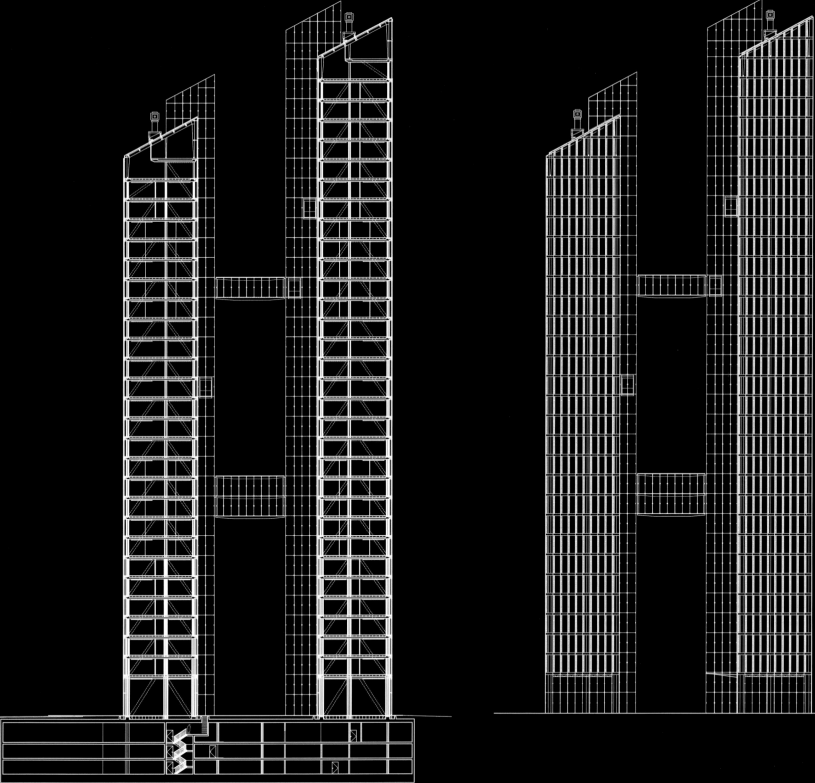

SKYLINE TOWER

Munich, Germany
Design 2001/Completion 2004
Client: Bayerische Hausbau
Helmut Jahn/Werner Sobek/Matthias Schuler

The Skyline Tower development marks the northern end of the Parkstadt Schwabing in Munich. It is the complementary project to the Hochhausensemble am Münchner Tor. This commission resulted also from an invited competition.

The five buildings follow closely the parameters of the urban plan. They are like extrusions with varying heights and create open und covered spaces with gardens and plazas in between.

The highest 'extrusion' is the tower which establishes, with its cantilevering roof, the 'skyline'. Below it, a 3-story skygarden reinforces the top and creates user-amenities.

The façades with a wide 2.7 m module are fully glazed with horizontal bands of stainless steel at the slab-edges allowing fresh-air intake for the decentralized conditioning system. Besides the wider module the difference to MAX and Hochhausensemble am Münchner Tor are glazed panels of sun-protective glass at the operable windows, which provide sun, wind, rain, acoustic and safety protection.

Triple- und double glazing, integrated heating and cooling, fan assisted convectors and centralized exhaust are applied consistent with the experience and know-how on previous projects.

The roof uses the prefabricated cells developed on Flughafen Köln/Bonn, Bayer and Deutsche Post. They regulate daylight and serve as weather and acoustic protection and provide insulation, drainage and room acoustics. A suspended cooled ceiling compensates for the higher solar loads due to the skylights.

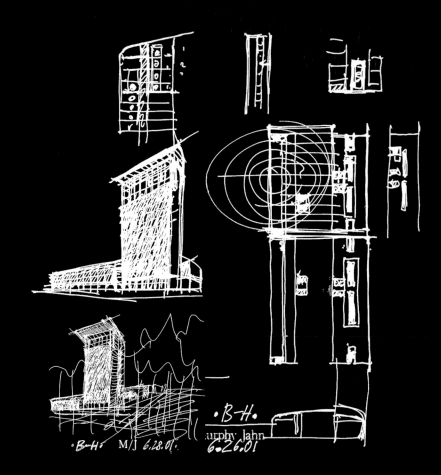

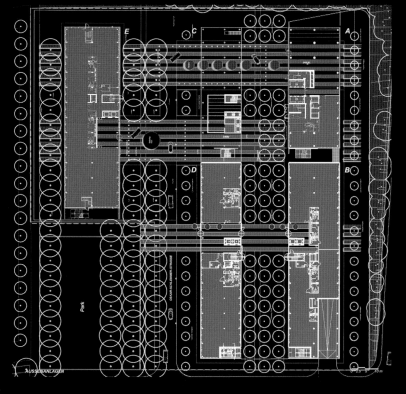

TRUMP TOWER

Stuttgart, Germany
Design 2002
Client: Trump Deutschland
Helmut Jahn/Werner Sobek/Matthias Schuler

With this entry to an invited ‚façade' competition we expanded the scope to propose a tall, transparent and ecological tower, which should become a new sign for Stuttgart, as a pendant to the Television Tower. Though unsuccessful in convincing the City and the developer, the project has lead to technical innovations, which will serve subsequent projects.

The round shape gives the tower an omnidirectional appearance on these hills. Its slanted void points towards City Hall, houses public functions and reinforces the intend to merge the top in such an ethereal way with the sky.

The multi-use with hotel, offices and apartments required a flexible structure and core-layout. This led to the 'exoskeleton' which carries vertical and all wind-loads through a steel tube-structure, keeping the core-wall thin and flexible in a 225 m high building. The double glazed façade is flush with the inside of the frame. Around the perimeter vertical shingles of heat-absorbing glass are bracketed off the slab edges providing sun, wind, rain, acoustic and safety protection and accommodating natural ventilation. They are oriented away from the prevailing south-west winds. The space between the outer and inner shells is used at hotel and apartments for balconies, terraces and wintergardens and supplies the air to the decentralized fan-assisted convectors, which support the integrated heating and cooling in the slabs. This system is a simplified version of the twin-shell system developed for Bayer and Deutsche Post. Its total reduction to frameless glass-panels gives the building its lightness and dematerialization.

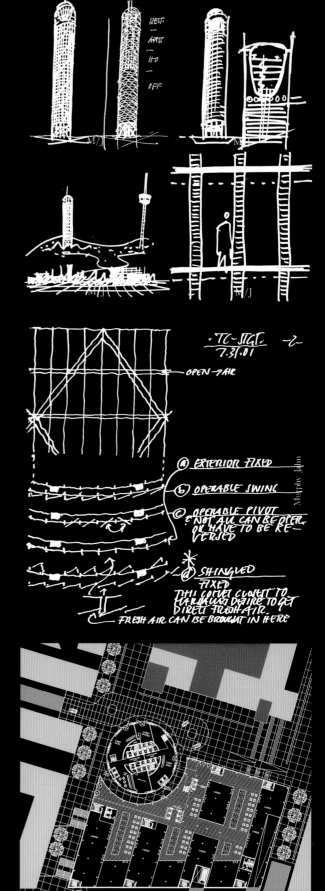

Trump Tower

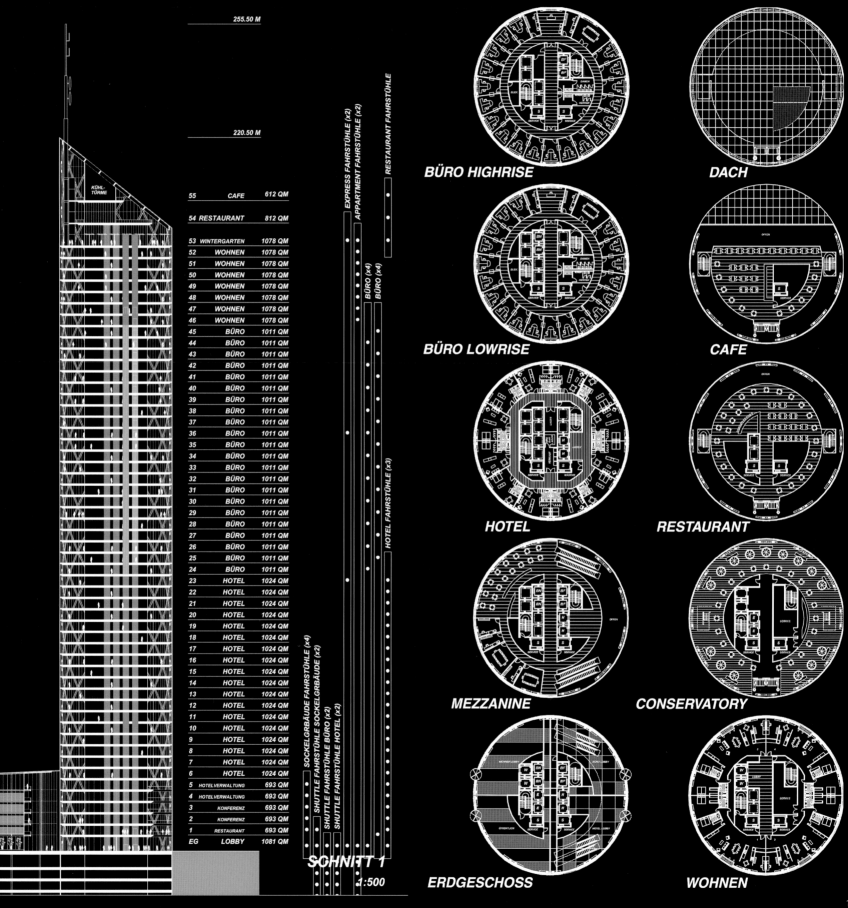

255.50 M

220.50 M

KÜHL-
TÜRME

55	CAFE	612 QM
54	RESTAURANT	812 QM
53	WINTERGARTEN	1078 QM
52	WOHNEN	1078 QM
51	WOHNEN	1078 QM
50	WOHNEN	1078 QM
49	WOHNEN	1078 QM
48	WOHNEN	1078 QM
47	WOHNEN	1078 QM
46	WOHNEN	1078 QM
45	BÜRO	1011 QM
44	BÜRO	1011 QM
43	BÜRO	1011 QM
42	BÜRO	1011 QM
41	BÜRO	1011 QM
40	BÜRO	1011 QM
39	BÜRO	1011 QM
38	BÜRO	1011 QM
37	BÜRO	1011 QM
36	BÜRO	1011 QM
35	BÜRO	1011 QM
34	BÜRO	1011 QM
33	BÜRO	1011 QM
32	BÜRO	1011 QM
31	BÜRO	1011 QM
30	BÜRO	1011 QM
29	BÜRO	1011 QM
28	BÜRO	1011 QM
27	BÜRO	1011 QM
26	BÜRO	1011 QM
25	BÜRO	1011 QM
24	BÜRO	1011 QM
23	HOTEL	1024 QM
22	HOTEL	1024 QM
21	HOTEL	1024 QM
20	HOTEL	1024 QM
19	HOTEL	1024 QM
18	HOTEL	1024 QM
17	HOTEL	1024 QM
16	HOTEL	1024 QM
15	HOTEL	1024 QM
14	HOTEL	1024 QM
13	HOTEL	1024 QM
12	HOTEL	1024 QM
11	HOTEL	1024 QM
10	HOTEL	1024 QM
9	HOTEL	1024 QM
8	HOTEL	1024 QM
7	HOTEL	1024 QM
6	HOTEL	1024 QM
5	HOTELVERWALTUNG	693 QM
4	HOTELVERWALTUNG	693 QM
3	KONFERENZ	693 QM
2	KONFERENZ	693 QM
1	RESTAURANT	693 QM
EG	LOBBY	1081 QM

SOCKELGRBÄUDE FAHRSTÜHLE (x4)
SHUTTLE FAHRSTÜHLE SOCKELGRBÄUDE (x2)
SHUTTLE FAHRSTÜHLE BÜRO (x2)
SHUTTLE FAHRSTÜHLE HOTEL (x2)
HOTEL FAHRSTÜHLE (x3)
BÜRO (x4)
BÜRO (x4)
EXPRESS FAHRSTÜHLE (x2)
APPARTMENT FAHRSTÜHLE (x2)
RESTAURANT FAHRSTÜHLE

SCHNITT 1

1:500

BÜRO HIGHRISE

DACH

BÜRO LOWRISE

CAFE

HOTEL

RESTAURANT

MEZZANINE

CONSERVATORY

ERDGESCHOSS

WOHNEN

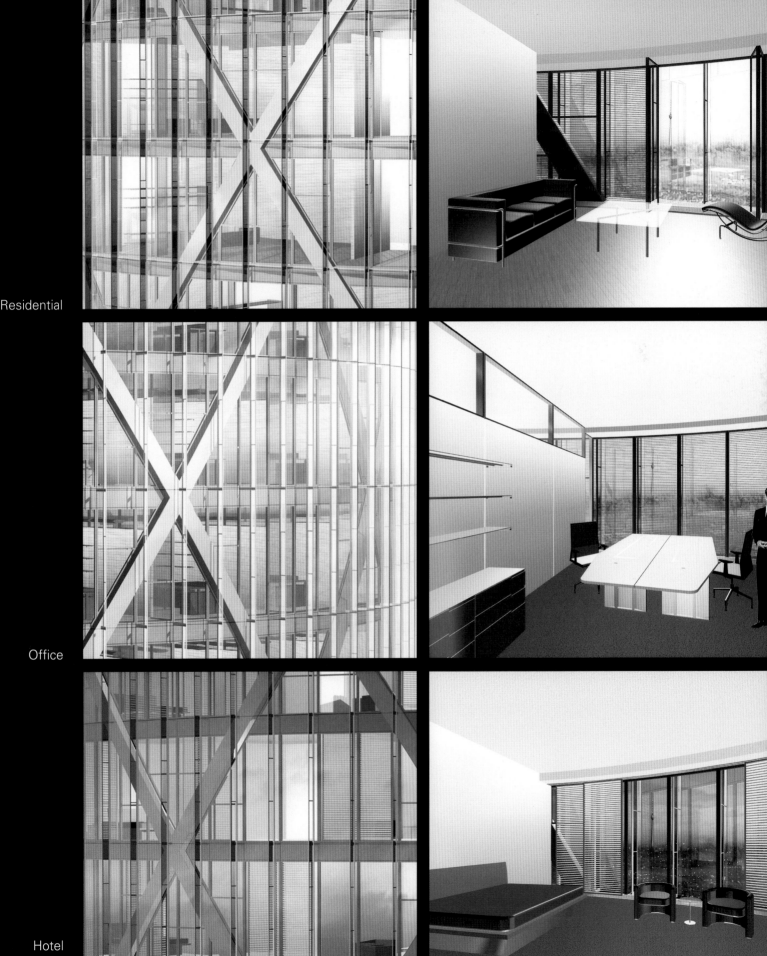

Residential

Office

Hotel

Helmut Jahn/Werner Sobek/Matthias Schuler

In an invited competition a solution was sought to replace a building by Egon Eiermann, which has become technically and functionally obsolete and needed major rehab to its façade, with a new structure.

The irregular curved shape responds to the angles of the surrounding buildings and streets. This leads to different lease-span configurations and enables multiple tenant configurations and a variety of office layouts.

The exterior envelope adapts the system developed for the circular Trump Tower which is suited well for this irregular, rounded wall. The structural concrete frame is located between the vertical exterior glass shingles and flush with the double-glazed façade providing office spaces free of perimeter columns. The wall is like a glass-curtain optimizing the views and strengthening the urban connections through transparency, reflections and its dynamic.

The energy-comfort concept uses the previously developed decentralized and integrated heating and cooling systems.

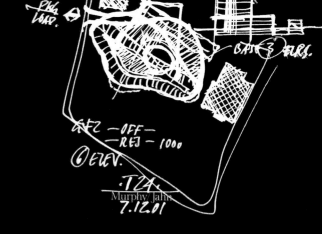

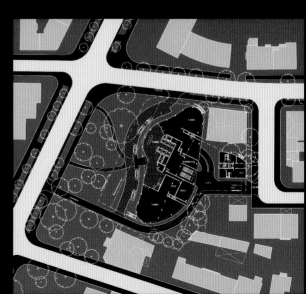

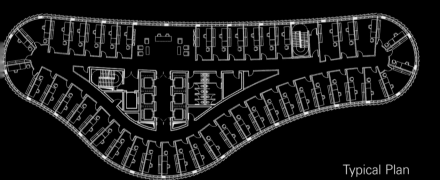

Typical Plan

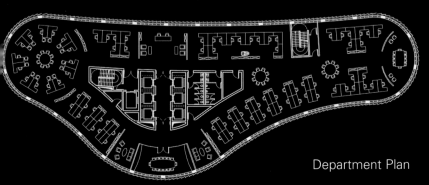

Department Plan

BRISTOL TOWN CENTER

Costa Mesa, California
Design 2000
Client: C. J. Segerstrom & Sons
Helmut Jahn / Werner Sobek

This project solidifies and expands the high-end market presence of an already prestigious commercial campus. The all glass façade maximizes the far views to the Pacific Ocean, whereas some of the less attractive immediate views are supplanted by the structurally incorporated gardens.

In difference to the European projects this is a completely sealed building resulting from the tenant expectations of the US-market, but also due to the relatively large lease-spans and the Californian climate. The building envelope will incorporate high performance low-E coating on the inner pane with a heat absorbing substrate at the outer light. Exhaust air will be at the window heads to extract heat gain at the source, without affecting the air system. The use of an underfloor displacement-system is still under study, pending the resolution of code- and tenant division issues.

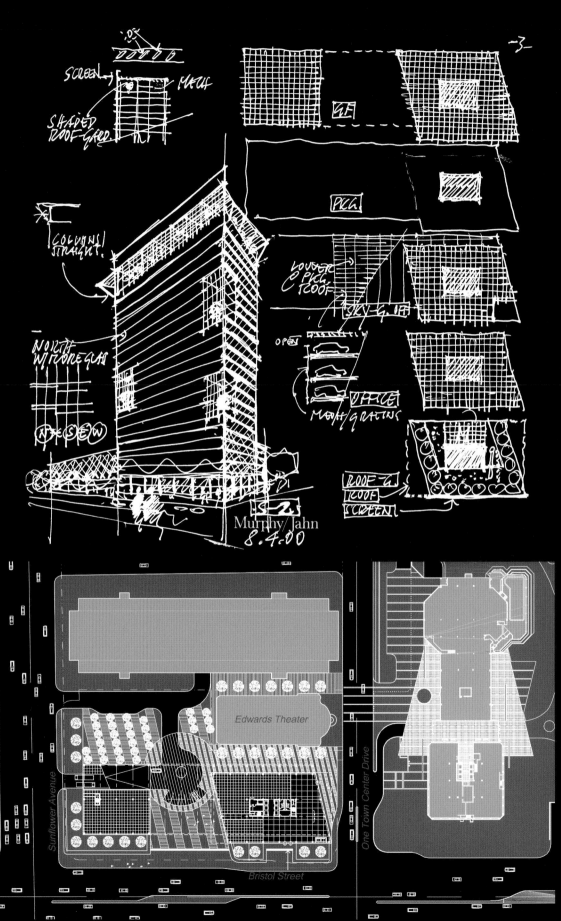

MANN

Chicago, Illinois
Design 2001
Client: Sunbelt Realty
Helmut Jahn/Werner Sobek

We submitted two schemes for this project in a limited competition.

What makes the MANN project particularly interesting is, that it adjoins one of those postmodern buildings of the 90's, which echo the style and materials of the Beaux Arts area of the 20's and 30's. The existing NBC Tower is edgy and stepped, MANN is tightly curved and straight, NBC is stone, MANN is glass, NBC is an isotropic layering of slabs, MANN is spatial and more open and responsive to its context and surroundings. MANN is bold and strong in the best Chicago tradition. It is contextual, responsive and functional, effective and flexible, technically innovative, ecologically responsive and pleasant and comfortable for its occupants.

The two schemes explore different relationships with the NBC-Tower and the urban context. The bow-shaped rectangle plays on NBC's basic geometry and offers different faces to the city and to the lake. The rounded square contrasts NBC even more and due to its height sets up an omnidirectional presence in the urban context which is further strengthened by its transparent luminous lantern with its slightly domed roof.

At the base the 'bow' continues NBC's circulation, whereas the 'square' sets up a separate identity with its lobby.

With regard to systems and materials similar strategies are applied like at Bristol Town Center, due to the same requirements and the added condition of dealing with the extreme climate differential between the Chicago summers and winters.

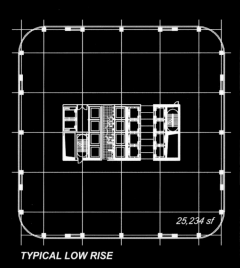

TYPICAL LOW RISE

25,234 sf

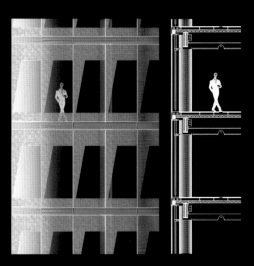

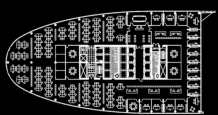

TYPICAL LOW RISE-SINGLE TENANT

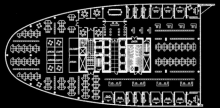

TYPICAL HIGH RISE-SINGLE TENANT

CANARY WHARF – NORTH QUAY

London, UK
Design 2001
Client: Canary Wharf Group PLC
Helmut Jahn/Werner Sobek

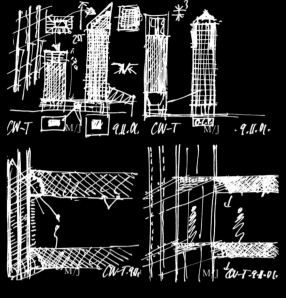

We were commissioned for this design study along with other practices.

North Quay offers the opportunity and challenge to create a grouping of strong architectural relationship, yet also distinct identity. The sloped top of the tall West Tower comes from introducing a new form yet with relationship to One Canada Square. The high point looks towards the City of London and becomes the front. By setting the floors back from the exterior glass-screen the Top becomes truly transparent and clearly distinct from the shaft, whose transparency is shallower. Both buildings distinguish clearly between base, shaft and top. Base and shaft are similar, the tops are different. The tall tower has a more assertive sloped top. The low East Tower is flat, with a glazed roof which curves into a rooftop courtyard, a "hidden" jewel.

The shafts of both buildings are fully glazed, except for protruding vertical mullions. They make the buildings viewed from different angles glassier or more solid and distinguish how the two buildings are perceived.

Most important to the ultimate appearance of the buildings is the concept of its transparent façade. What we are talking about here is not a see-through building, but a façade which reveals its different layers of surface, shades, slab edge and ceiling in multiple ways at day and night.

The structural and mechanical systems follow the standards established for Canary Wharf which have served the development very well and established high levels of comfort and flexibility for tenants in a sealed building. With floor areas exceeding 3000 m² , the use of daylight and fresh air is out of the question and of minimal influence in the total energy budget of the buildings. If there is room for improvement it is through development of more efficient glass and shading systems and their individual or central control.

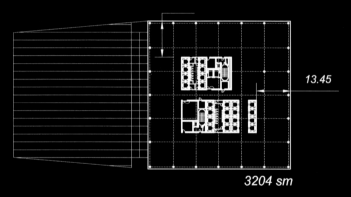

13.45

3204 sm

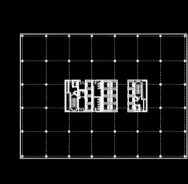

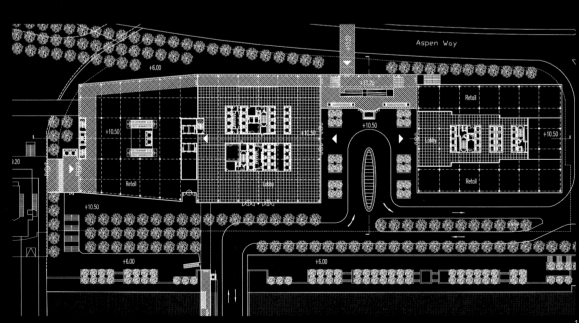

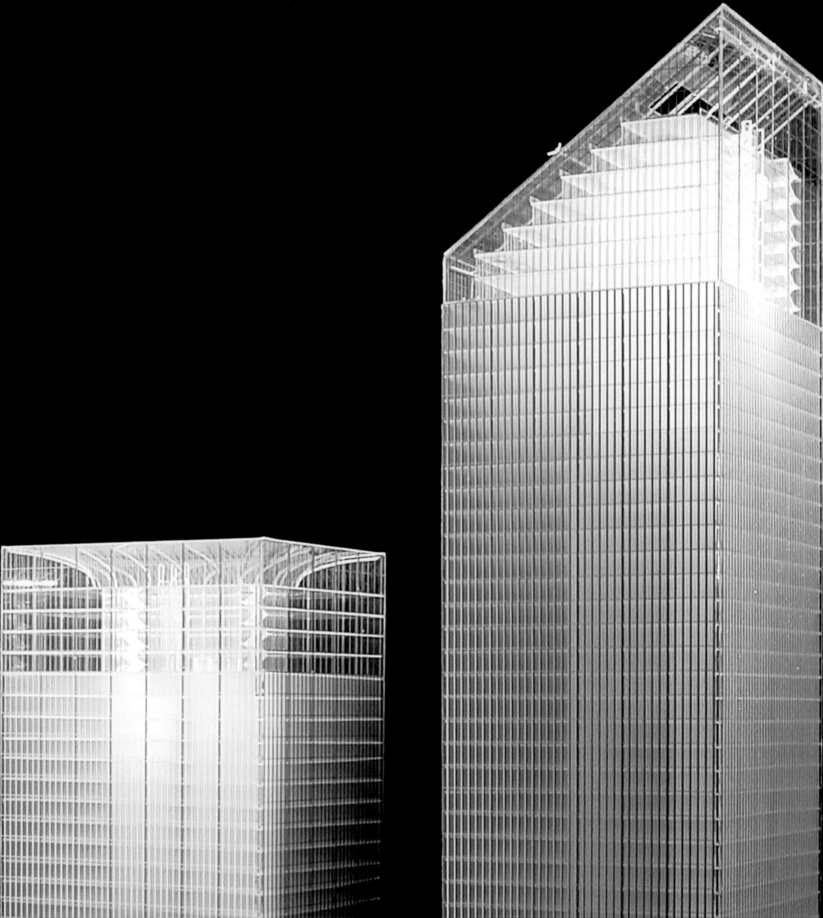

Façade

Façade elevation section

S-TOKYO

Tokyo, Japan
Design 2001
Client: Mitsubishi Estate Co., Ltd.
Helmut Jahn/Werner Sobek

A simple and bold strategy was adopted to give the building a special presence. Various layered screens of glass define the building's volume and distinguish between base and tower and give those parts a clear and crisp definition. The east and west faces of the tower are eroded in either an angular or a curved geometry. This gives those primary façades a recognizable and distinct image. Beyond that, the screen and the space between the screen and the façades serves other goals. Narrow balconies projecting into this zone allow to step outside and enjoy the views of the Imperial Palace and the city.

The façade of the building is glazed with floor-to-floor, high performance insulated glass panels with a Low-E coating. The screen wall is designed to act as a solar screen eliminating 65 % of the solar gain on these façades.

The layered screens dematerialize the building and the base and thus render the building in many intriguing ways. The glass changes from transparent to opaque, based on viewing and light conditions. Signs and images can be projected, screened or mounted on these glass walls and portray messages and communicate with the viewer from the outside and thus improve the marketing potential. The coated glass screen also becomes an exterior sun protection for the east and the critical west façades. Horizontal slots at each floor, together with the open north and south ends assure sufficient air movements to avoid heat build-up.

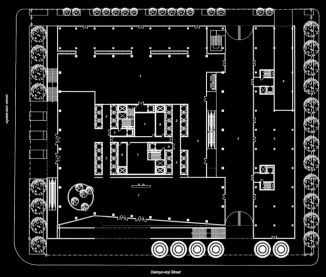

Daimyo-koji Street

Steel Bracket
Build-Up T-section

Stainless Steel Profiled Cladding

Insulated Glass Panels
w/Low-E Coating

100 mm Perforated
Blinds

Insulated Glass Roof

Extruded Aluminum
Profile

Steel Fin

Single Glazed
Laminated,
Heat-Absorbing
Glass Solar Screen

Single Glazed Handrail

Ventilation Slots

Laminated Glass Floor

Outside

Stainless Steel Balcony Grille

10 cms Raised Floor

1.30 mts

2.80 mts

4.20 mts

70 cms Steel Column

40 cms

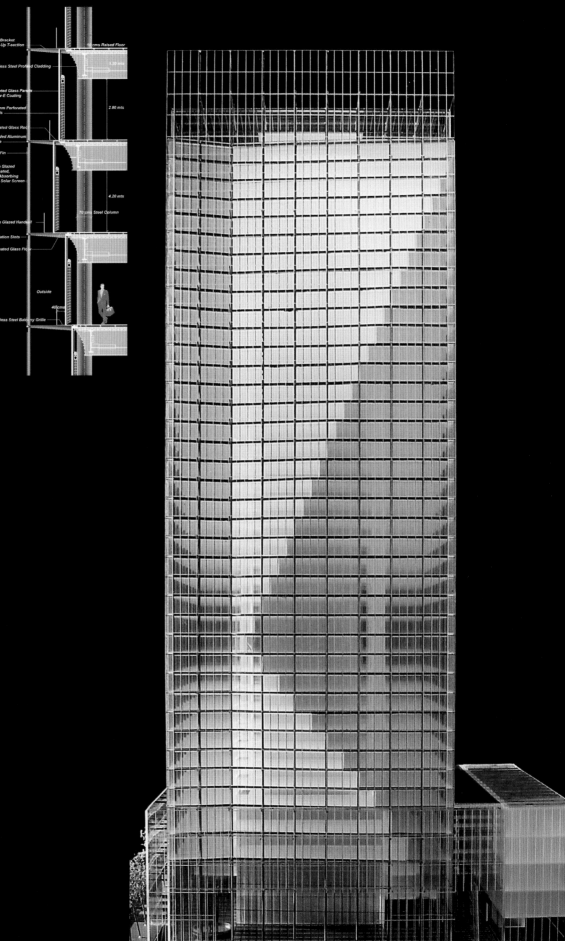

TORRE ESPACIO HIGH-RISE

Madrid, Spain
Design 2002
Client: Torre Espacio Castellana
Helmut Jahn/Werner Sobek/Matthias Schuler

The invited competition was held for what is going to become the tallest building in Madrid.

Torre Espacio assumes this responsibility to become a clearly recognizable symbol for the city. We opted for a building of utmost simplicity, elegance, and 'contained' beauty to make a strong statement. Torre Espacio responds to these goals as a tall, slender obelisk with a lantern top of two different alternate configurations to address the greater urban environs.

The clear plan leads to a simple and efficient structure. The shear-walls of the core are connected at the middle and top of the building with 3-story diagonal, cross-shaped outriggers to the exterior columns using their tension and compression capacity to resist the lateral forces. The building is without interior and corner-columns.

The fully glazed façade assures maximum day lighting and views. Operable parts in the wall facilitate natural ventilation of the offices. Incorporated into the façade is also the night lighting system and an innovative way how the shading system can also accommodate the requirement of a fire-spandrel in a fully glazed façade.

Due to Madrid's high summer temperatures a decentralized air-system is not feasible, due to even higher temperatures at the façade surface. This lead to the selection of a cooled ceiling for basic conditioning with a centralized system distributing the air along the displacement principle from the floor.

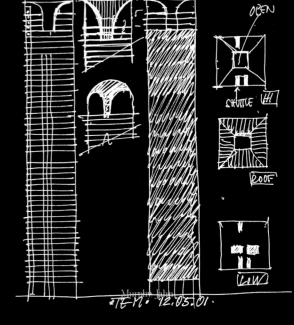

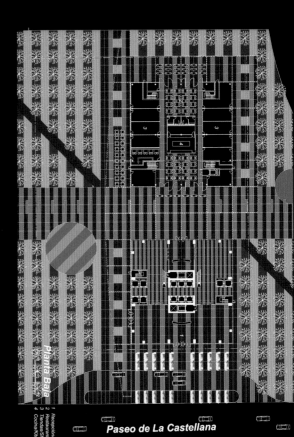

Planta Baja

Paseo de La Castellana

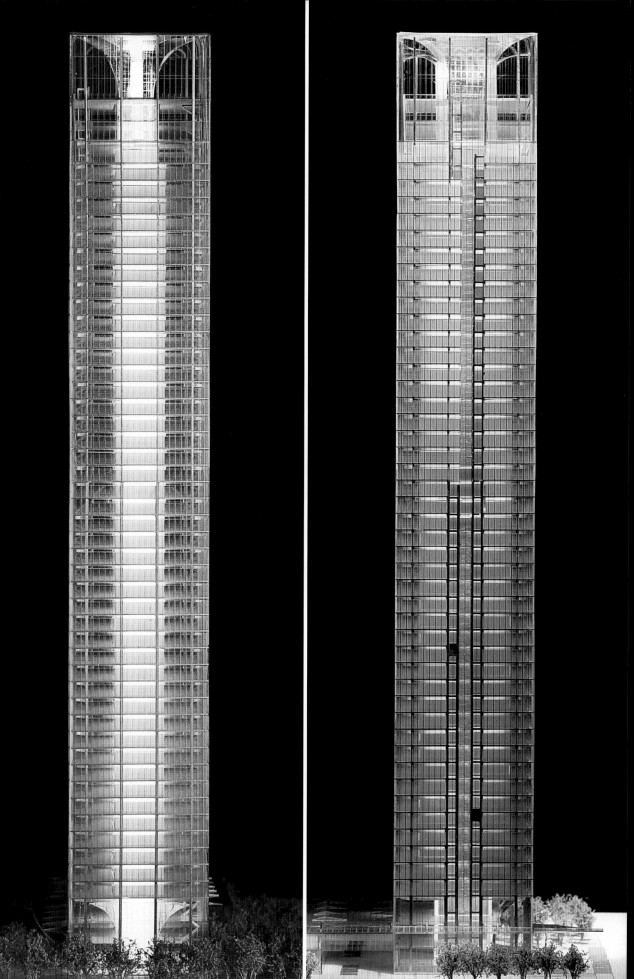

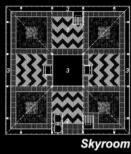

Skyroom

1 Sky Room
2 Terraza/Sky Terrace
3 Vestíbulo de Ascensores/
Elevator Lobby
4 Doble altura/
Open to Below

Piso 45

1 Recepción/Lobby
2 Lavabos/Toilet Rooms
3 Oficinas Ejecutivas/
Executive Offices
4 Balcón/Balcony
5 Sala de Juntas/
Meeting Room
6 Doble altura/
Open to Below

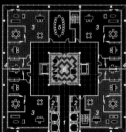

Piso 44

1 Recepción/Lobby
2 Lavabos/Toilet Rooms
3 Oficinas Ejecutivas/
Executive Offices
4 Balcón/Balcony
5 Sala de Juntas/
Meeting Room
6 Patio Escultórico/
Sculptural Court

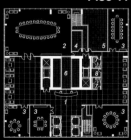

**Piso 43
Sala de Consejo/
Piso de Transferencia**

1 Recepción/Lobby
2 Sala de Consejo/
Board Room
3 Comedor/Dining Rooms
4 Audio Visual/
AV Room
5 Cocineta/
Food Prepararion
6 Cuárto de Máquinas de
Ascensores/
Elevator Machine Room
7 Lavabos/Toilet Rooms
8 Cuártos de Máquinas/
Mech Rooms

0   4   8   12

1465 m²   Centro de Conferencias/ Puente

1296 m²   Planta Baja

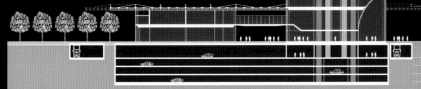

TOKYO STATION YAESU REDEVELOPMENT

Tokyo, Japan
Design 2002/Completion 2010
Client: East Japan Railway Co.; Mitsui Fudosan
Co., Ltd.; Kokusai Kanko Kaikan Co., Ltd.;
Kajima Yaesu Kaihatsu Co., Ltd.;
Nippon Mitsubishi Oil Corp.; Yaesu Auto-
Service Co., Ltd.
Design Architect: Murphy/Jahn
Helmut Jahn/Werner Sobek
Architects and Engineers: Nikken Sekkei Ltd.
JR East Design Corporation JV

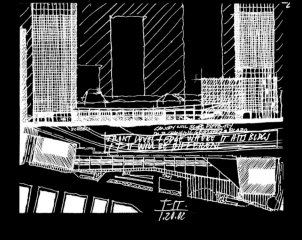

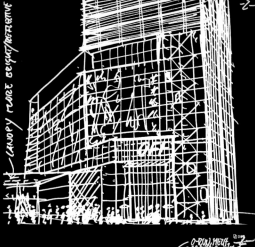

Through an invited competition we were selected as design architect for one of the largest and most important projects in central Tokyo. The 200 m height of the buildings and the basic massing was established by the planning criteria and the physical restrictions of a tight site.

The central part gives Tokyo-Station a new entry. Whereas the historic station to the west is traditional, the new entry is dynamic and technical and the towers are fully glazed and become transparent, reflective or lit beacons at night. The tops of the towers turn through their double-shell façades into luminous lanterns reinforcing this intent. The North-Tower sits on a 12-story department store. Its façade of translucent and clear glass allows for signage and display of advertisement and products.

The large footprints of the towers exceed 4000 m² and lease spans vary from 16 to 27 m depending on core-configurations and are mostly column-free.

Like the buildings in Germany or the United States the convention of construction is inescapable in determining the buildings' systems and components. In terms of structure it is seismic design and for conditioning it is Tokyo's hot and humid summer climate, which is of primary influence and lead to the choice of steel and a sealed envelope.

The 'airflow-façade' is an innovative response to the energy- and comfort parameters. It can be considered a mechanized version of the German twin-shell façades which operate with natural airflow. The sealed exterior skin is of single, clear uncoated glass. A second sheet of the same glass is on the inside with blinds in the 15 cm air-space. Through a slot at the base of the interior shell exhaust air from the space is drawn to the head of the window, extracting the heat gain at the source, with no negative effect on the room temperature. Further studies are in progress to assess the increased costs of such envelope in relation to the savings in mechanical systems, operational savings and resultant increased user comfort.

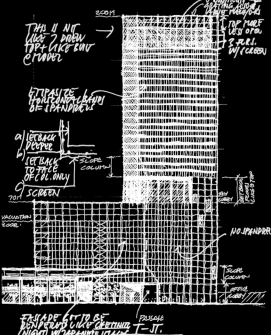

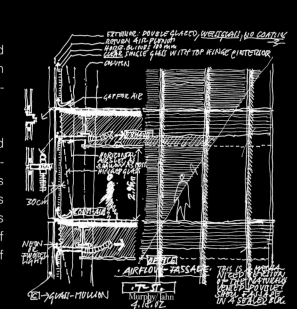

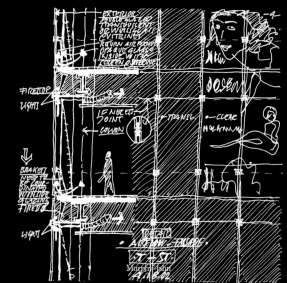

HAFEN – DÜSSELDORF

Düsseldorf, Germany
Design 2002/Completion 2005
Client: Frankonia Eurobau AG
Helmut Jahn/Werner Sobek/Matthias Schuler

The development of the old Rhine harbor into a modern business district is an important urban project in Düsseldorf. It is known as Media-hafen and already built up to a large extent with very individualistic buildings.

The primary intention of the project is therefore to counter the variety of forms and colors with a building of great simplicity, elegance and identity. It should not convince through form and style, but through the quality of the materials, the flexibility in its use and the high comfort it offers the users. Through its technology and construction it should advance the typology of the office block.

The plan is a 'Roundangle' whose curved corners continue to form a semi-circular roof. Elevators and stairs are in a separate rectangle of glass. Columns with brackets along the exterior wall enable column-free spaces in the office areas.

The shingled façade is more than the building envelope. It is an integral part of the energy/comfort concept and becomes the expression of its optimization and the ecological goals. Its aesthetic and configuration are the result of a serious and scientific pursuit of these goals.

The overlapping sheets of insulating glass form the shingled surface. At the offset at the slab edge decentralized air is brought directly into the room as fresh air through an operating sash, or cooled and heated through water in a fan-assisted convector and distributed as displacement air. Through the basic system of integrated heating and cooling in the concrete slabs, air-changes are kept to a minimum, return airshafts are reduced, and no supply shafts are needed with the decentralized air-system. The façade is allowed to 'breathe'. The building acts like a natural skin, therefore, conventional operable windows are not necessary.

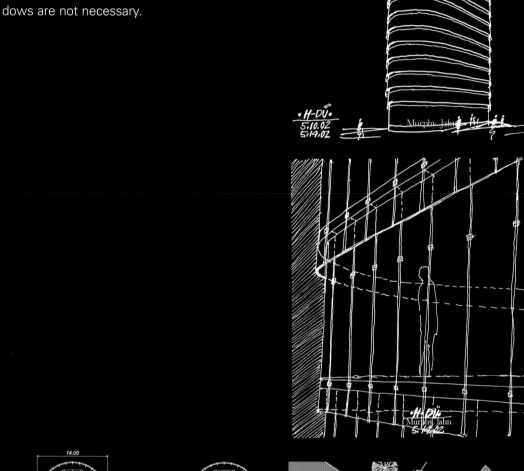

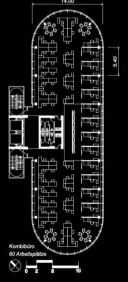

Kombibüro
60 Arbeitsplätze

Großraumbüro
75 Arbeitsplätze

Typische Geschosse

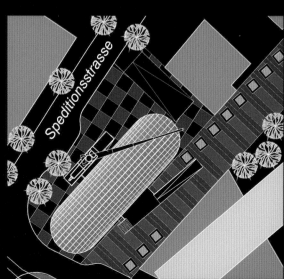

HEGAU TOWER

Singen, Germany
Design 2002/Completion 2005
Client: GVV Städtische Wohnbaugesellschaft
Singen mbh
Helmut Jahn/Werner Sobek

The small town of Singen near Lake Constance is changing from its manufacturing base to attract the service industry. Hegau Tower is intended as a statement for this change.

The project has to be very competitive and fit the projected rental market. This led us to the design of a simple long rectangle, which changes in height to form the tower. This linearity is reinforced through the projecting glass-screens and the stairs and balconies at the building's short ends.

The simple form led to a clear structure, a tight all-glass façade and a further optimized energy/comfort system. In order to reduce the technical equipment further, exterior shading is necessary at the long southwest façade. At the northwest and southeast, improved glazing is able to reduce the solar-loads. The basic conditioning is done with integrated heating and cooling in the concrete slabs. In order to facilitate controllable fresh air, operable offset flaps at the slab-edge facilitate supply and exhaust. A continuous convector prevents draft from falling cold air in winter and heats fresh air, allowing for natural ventilation also by extreme cold outside temperatures. Special tenant wishes for higher comfort can be accommodated by exchanging the regular convectors with fan-assisted units for heating and cooling.

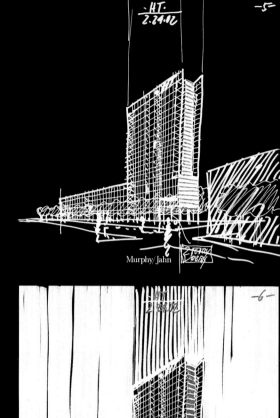

Murphy/Jahn

Murphy/Jahn
Murphy/Jahn

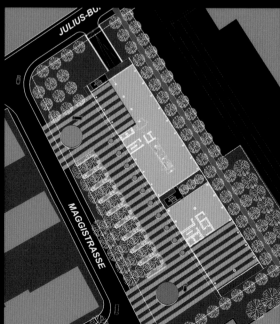

NEW BANGKOK INTERNATIONAL AIRPORT

Bangkok, Thailand
Design 1995/Completion 2005
Client: New Bangkok Int'l Airport Co., Ltd.
Helmut Jahn/Werner Sobek/Matthias Schuler
MJTA Consortium
Murphy/Jahn/Tams/ACT

NBIA resulted from an International Competition and established the basis of collaboration between Werner Sobek, Matthias Schuler and Helmut Jahn. The challenge was great and unusual. The task of creating a new gateway to Thailand in a tropical climate necessitated a different approach to architecture and engineering. Through the integration of the disciplines the complex problem resulted in a sophisticated, intelligent yet simple solution. After five years of planning and procurement the airport is now under construction and set to open for passenger traffic in early 2005.

NBIA is one of the largest airports in the world with 500 000 m² and 60 wide body gates. The arrival and departure halls are totally glazed and the arched concourses combine glass and membrane to form a 'macrostructure' for varying circulation patterns and uses. A large trellis roof shades the glazed terminal building and part of the concourses and becomes the recognizable gesture and identity for the city and the country. It extends beyond the enclosed spaces to cover gardens, which represent city or country and introduces arriving passengers to the jungle of the tropics.

The integration of architecture and engineering accomplishes that every part serves more than its conventional role. Steel and concrete structures, glass or membrane roofs and the glazed façades are fully integrated systems, serving architectural, structural and environmental parameters. In the course of the design new composite glass-types and a three-layer, translucent membrane were developed to mediate between exterior and interior conditions, dealing with noise transmission and heat,

while still allowing for natural daylight within. The combination of glass and roof with a cooled floor system ensures the comfort and reduces the installed cooling power to 60 % of a conventional conditioning system.

NBIA best represents the goal to construct buildings where nothing must be added and nothing can be taken away.

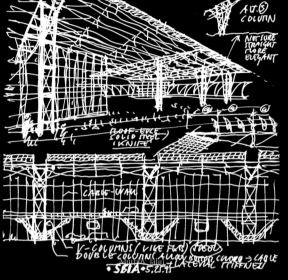

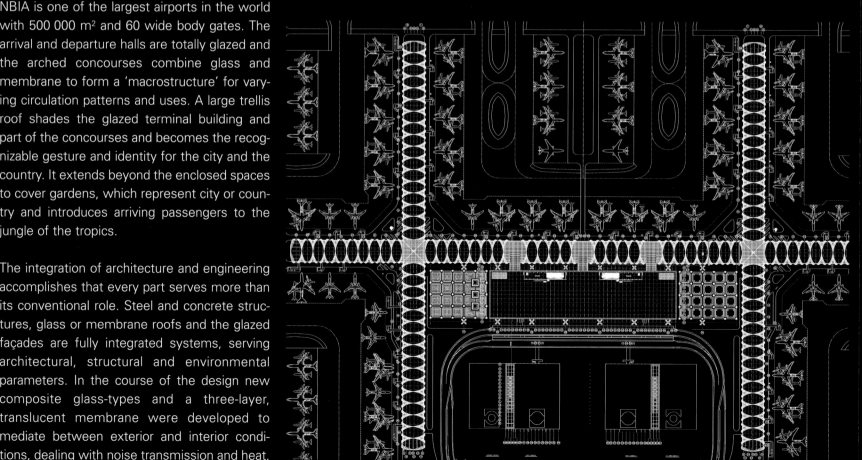

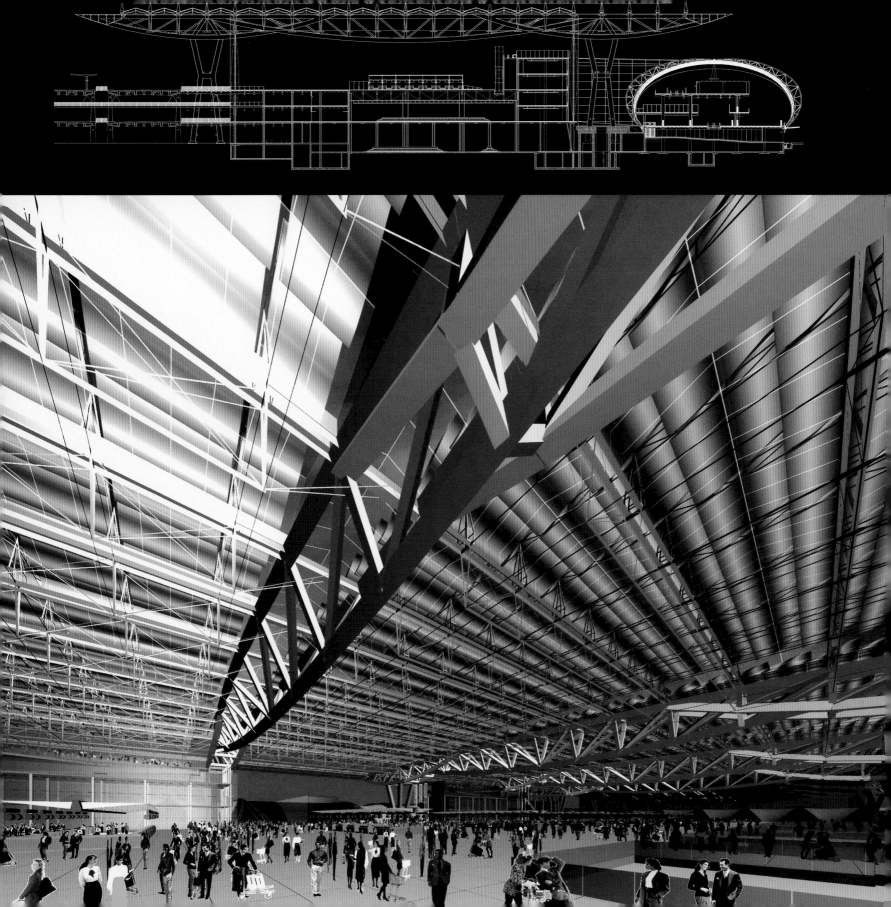

Concourse space truss girders

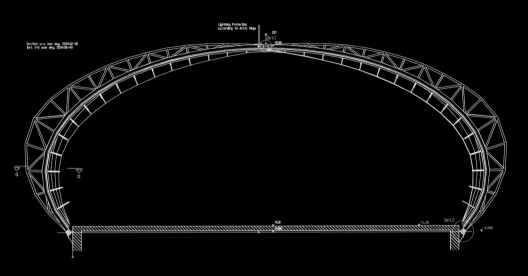

Section a-s see dwg. 5204.02-00
Det. 1+2 see dwg. 5204.06-00

Lightning Protection
according to Arch. Dwgs

Det.1

Det.2

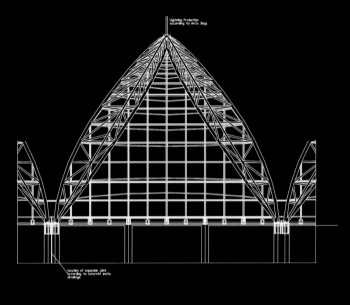

Lightning Protection
according to Arch. Dwgs

location of expansion joint
according to concrete works
drawings

Fabric not shown

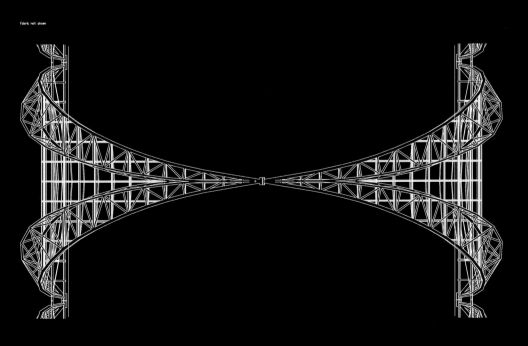

Fabric not shown

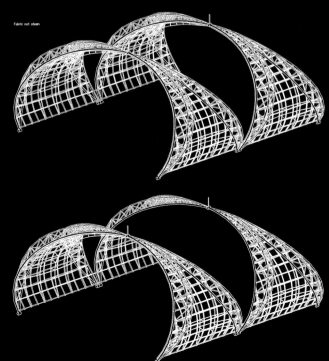

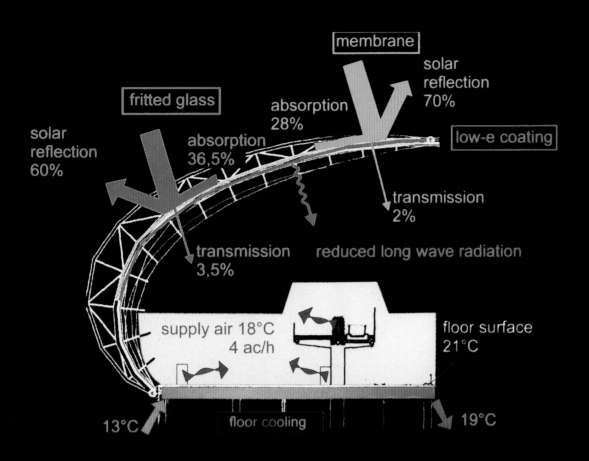

membrane

solar reflection 70%

fritted glass

solar reflection 60%

absorption 28%

absorption 36,5%

low-e coating

transmission 2%

transmission 3,5%

reduced long wave radiation

supply air 18°C 4 ac/h

floor surface 21°C

13°C

floor cooling

19°C

OPTIMIZED ENERGY CONCEPT CONCOURSES

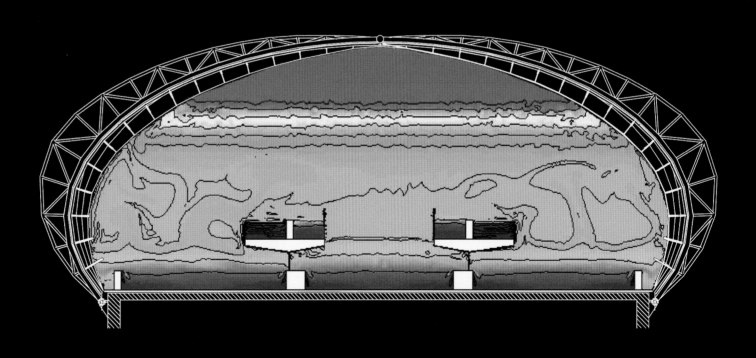

SHANGHAI INTERNATIONAL AIRPORT

Shanghai, China
Design 1998
Client: Shanghai Pudong Airport Corporation
Helmut Jahn/Werner Sobek

The underlying idea of this design in an International Airport Competition is to introduce structures related to airplanes to airports. Here the terminal is covered by a giant roof with winged cantilevers from fuselage-type beams, supported by inclined columns. The concourses like cross sections of planes are of cable-stayed arches, covered with solid or glass cells.

In the absence of a masterplan, Werner Sobek and I established this approach. The building becomes a statement of the power of an idea, using the know-how of previous developed technology regarding structure, enclosure and conditioning.

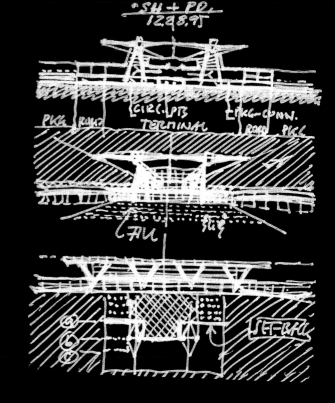

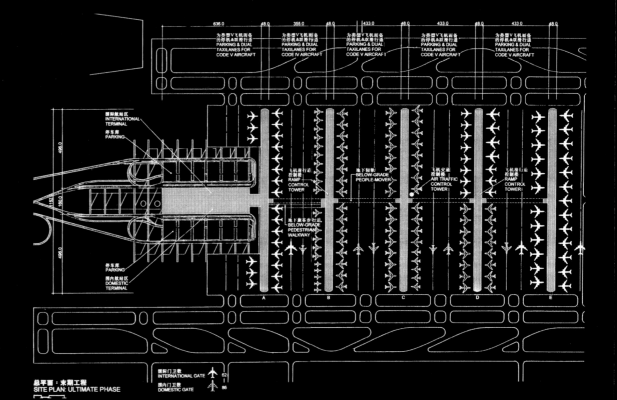

总平面：末期工程
SITE PLAN: ULTIMATE PHASE

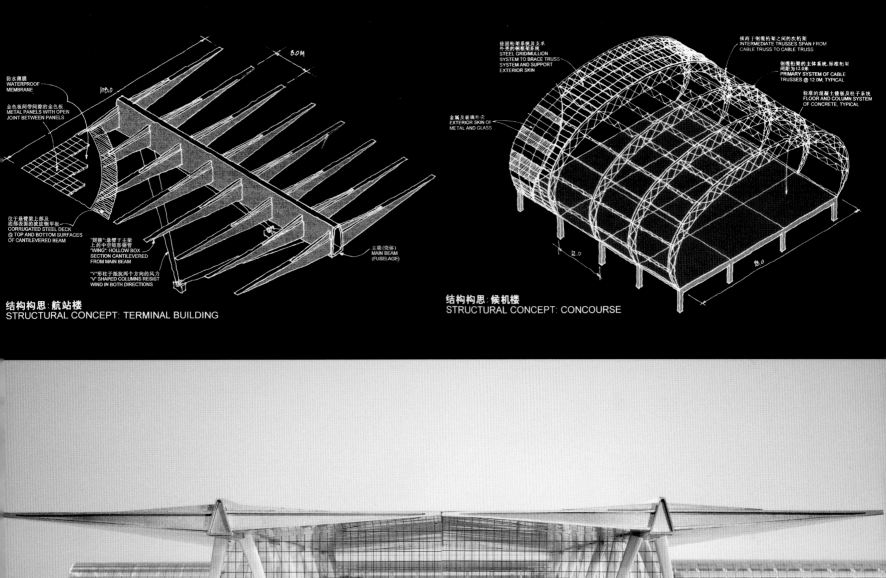

防水隔膜
WATERPROOF
MEMBRANE

金色板间间隙的金色板
METAL PANELS WITH OPEN
JOINT BETWEEN PANELS

位于悬臂梁上部及
底部表面的波纹倒甲板
CORRUGATED STEEL DECK
@ TOP AND BOTTOM SURFACES
OF CANTILEVERED BEAM

"翅膀":悬臂手主梁
上的中空矩形钢管
"WING": HOLLOW BOX
SECTION CANTILEVERED
FROM MAIN BEAM

"V"形柱子抵抗两个方向的风力
"V" SHAPED COLUMNS RESIST
WIND IN BOTH DIRECTIONS

主梁(壳体)
MAIN BEAM
(FUSELAGE)

8.0M
108.0

结构构思:航站楼
STRUCTURAL CONCEPT: TERMINAL BUILDING

锚固桁架系统及支承
外壳的钢框架系统
STEEL GRID/MULLION
SYSTEM TO BRACE TRUSS
SYSTEM AND SUPPORT
EXTERIOR SKIN

横跨于钢缆桁架之间的次桁架
INTERMEDIATE TRUSSES SPAN FROM
CABLE TRUSS TO CABLE TRUSS

钢缆桁架的主体系统,标准桁架
间距为12.0米
PRIMARY SYSTEM OF CABLE
TRUSSES @ 12.0M, TYPICAL

标准的混凝土楼板及柱子系统
FLOOR AND COLUMN SYSTEM
OF CONCRETE, TYPICAL

金属及玻璃外壳
EXTERIOR SKIN OF
METAL AND GLASS

12.0
18.0

结构构思:候机楼
STRUCTURAL CONCEPT: CONCOURSE

TERMINAL 2 MUNICH AIRPORT

Munich, Germany
Design 1998
Client: Flughafen München GmbH
Deutsche Lufthansa AG
Helmut Jahn/Werner Sobek/Matthias Schuler

Since 1988 we have been working at the new Munich Airport. The essential parts of the 'Airport City' are now complete with the Hotel Kempinski and the Airport Center. In 1998 an invited competition was held for Terminal 2, which completes the 'Airport City' to the east.

The MAC-Forum becomes the forecourt of Terminal 2 and its roof is expanded to create a closer linkage. This close entwinement between terminal and commercial uses, road, rail and air is unique among large airports around the world and reinforces the idea of the 'City outside the City'.

The systems proposed to explore the cutting edge of available technology. Switchable glass-cells in the roof, composite façade glazing on cable supports as well as integrated floor cooling and heating are all part of the overall strategy to maximize comfort and minimize technical equipment in a total glass building.

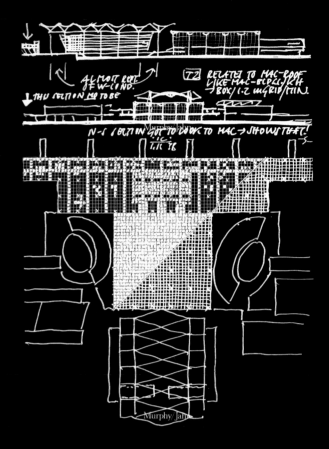

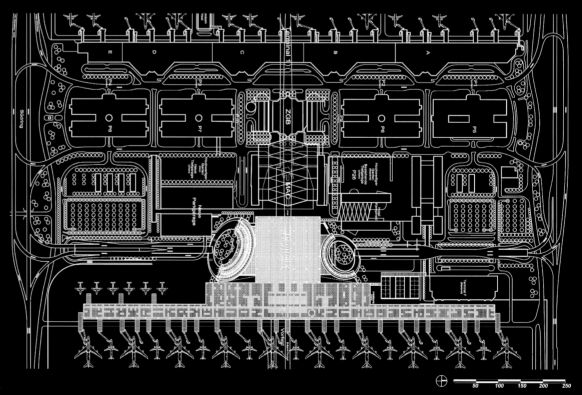

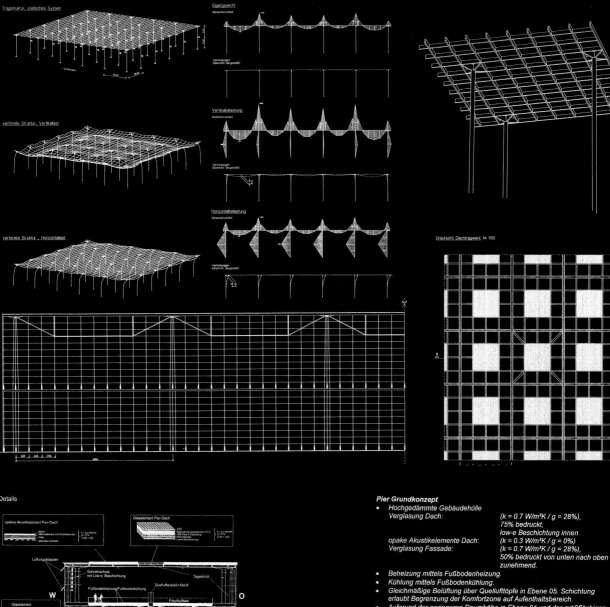

Details

Sommer

Winter

Pier Grundkonzept

- Hochgedämmte Gebäudehülle
  Verglasung Dach: (k = 0.7 W/m²K / g = 28%), 75% bedruckt, low-e Beschichtung innen
  opake Akustikelemente Dach: (k = 0.3 W/m²K / g = 0%)
  Verglasung Fassade: (k = 0.7 W/m²K / g = 28%), 50% bedruckt von unten nach oben zunehmend.
- Beheizung mittels Fußbodenheizung.
- Kühlung mittels Fußbodenkühlung.
- Gleichmäßige Belüftung über Quellufttöpfe in Ebene 05. Schichtung erlaubt Begrenzung der Komfortzone auf Aufenthaltsbereich.
- Aufgrund der geringeren Raumhöhe in Ebene 04 und der großflächigen Deckendurchbrüche zwischen Ebene 04 und 05 wird in Ebene 04 auf ein Quelluftsystem verzichtet. Belüftung über Mischluftsystem.
- Natürliche Belichtung in Ebene 05 über ausreichende transluzente Oberlichtanteile.
- Tiefe Tageslichtbereiche in Ebene 04 über offene Randstreifen.

Sommer

- Optimale Komfortbedingungen bei minimiertem Energieaufwand für Kühlung.
- Die Fußbodenkühlung transportiert die Strahlungsgewinne direkt ab. Gleichzeitig ergibt die kühle Oberfläche eine angenehme Empfindungstemperatur.
- Das Quelluftsystem verdrängt warme, verbrauchte Luft nach oben. Warme Luftschichten im Bereich der Dachverglasung müssen nicht konditioniert werden. Minimum an Kühlleistung für den wohltemperierten Aufenthaltsbereich.
- Geschlossene Glasbrüstungen halten den kühlen Frischluftsee in Ebene 05. Durchbrüche wie Rolltreppen werden lufttechnisch verschlossen.
- Low-e Schicht auf der Glasinnenseite verhindert infrarote Abstrahlung. Warme Dachverglasung hat damit keinen Einfluß auf Komfortbedingungen.
- Sonnenschutzbehänge an der Westfassade verhindern Komforteinbussen, durch direkte Solarstrahlung bzw. Blendung.
- Ablüften der Warmluftpolster im Dachbereich möglich.

Winter

- Ideale Komfortbedingungen durch gleichmäßige Beheizung über Flächenheizung (empfundene Temperatur höher als Lufttemperatur).
- Kein Einfluß der kälteren Dachverglasung auf die Empfindungstemperatur in Ebene 05, da low-e Schicht auf Glasinnenseite.
- Optimaler Schadstoffabtransport durch mechanische Belüftung über die Quellufttöpfe (Schichtlüftungsprinzip) in Ebene 05. Verbrauchte Luft wird nach oben verdrängt.
- Hochisolierende Verglasungselemente (k = 0.7 W/m²K) verhindern einen Kaltluftabfall an der Fassade und minimieren die Transmissionsverluste.

Terminal 2 Munich Airport

O'HARE FACE T1, T2, T3

O'Hare International Airport
Chicago, Illinois
Design 2001/Completion 2005
Client: City of Chicago, Department of Aviation
Helmut Jahn/Werner Sobek

Conceived and built nearly forty years ago, Chicago O'Hare International Airport provided an image of functionality attuned to the jet-age. As it grew to cope with ever increasing air traffic, airside facilities were expanded and adapted to the increased demands of the passengers, while landside improvements primarily addressed only vehicular demands. The functional clarity and unity of scale of the original complex were consequently lost. The Façade and Circulation Enhancement Project addresses this by utilizing principles based on actual experience on similar projects.

Technology and efficiency are also utilized in interior improvements, providing greater passenger comfort and improved lighting while reducing energy consumption and costs. The replacement of antiquated mechanical and air distribution systems leads to implement new ceiling and lighting technologies. New floor finishes, wall panels, railings, furnishings and landscape elements complete the interior transformation.

The new canopy, scaled to the expanded O'Hare, provides improved curbside protection while creating a unified identity for the airport. The expanded terminal space enables improved passenger circulation, greater visual clarity for passenger orientation and enhanced airline identification. The enclosure is minimal, clear and very efficient in its use of materials and technology.

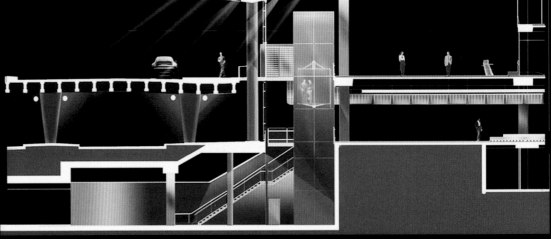

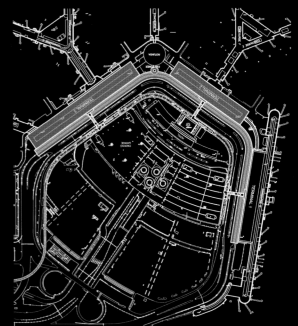

TRANSRAPID MAGNETSCHNELLBAHN

Germany
Design 1998
Client: Magnetschnellbahn Planungs-
gesellschaft mbH
Helmut Jahn/Werner Sobek/Matthias Schuler

The Transrapid is the fastest track-bound means of transportation with maximum speeds of up to 475 km/h. A test track is in operation in Lathen, Emsland. Implementation is planned between Berlin and Hamburg at a travel time of 59 minutes.

The Berlin station is in a tunnel adjacent to the Lehrter Bahnhof. The Hamburg station is adjacent to the Hauptbahnhof between the tracks. The three stations in-between are on the elevated guideway in Berlin-Potsdam, Schwerin and Hamburg-Moorfleet. The design for the Schwerin station establishes the systems and components, which are to be applied to the different conditions of all stations.

The MPG as builder and the Deutsche Bahn as operator were looking for representative architecture, which becomes an 'address' for the system. Emphasis was put onto easy connection to ground transportation and the existing short-range and long-range trains (ICE). The ease and movement of the customer had to be compatible with the speed of the train.

The design consists of three parts: the roof over the platform of the station with its integral structural, glazed wall protecting the passengers from the moving trains; the envelope of the distribution level with access to the existing train station and the street; the Transrapid becomes the third part, completing, together with roof and envelope, the total composition. The moving train is integrated and becomes an element of change.

The structure is derived from the guideway structure for the Transrapid. The distribution level is a cantilevered, bridge-like steel frame,

which carries, supported by light steel frames, an envelope of glass and metal panels. Curved spatial girders span 22 m between the main support columns, wrap around the guideways and continue to support the platform and its enclosure, the station platform and the curved roof, which cantilevers considerably at its ends.

The design integrates guideway, train, structure and enclosure into a total composition, which gives a clear reading of its parts and becomes the Transrapid's image.

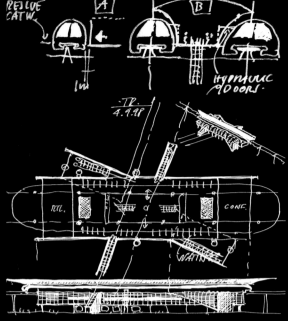

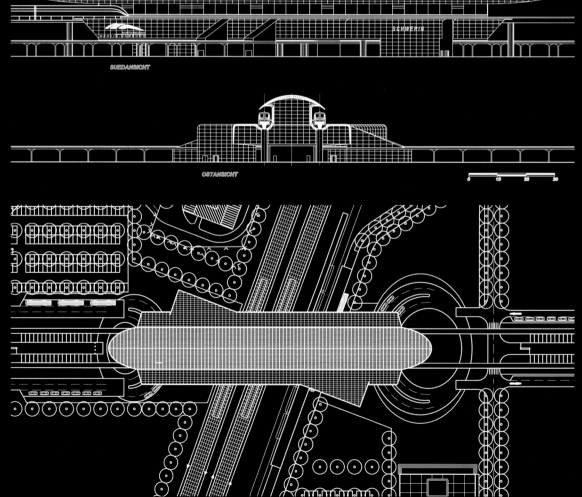

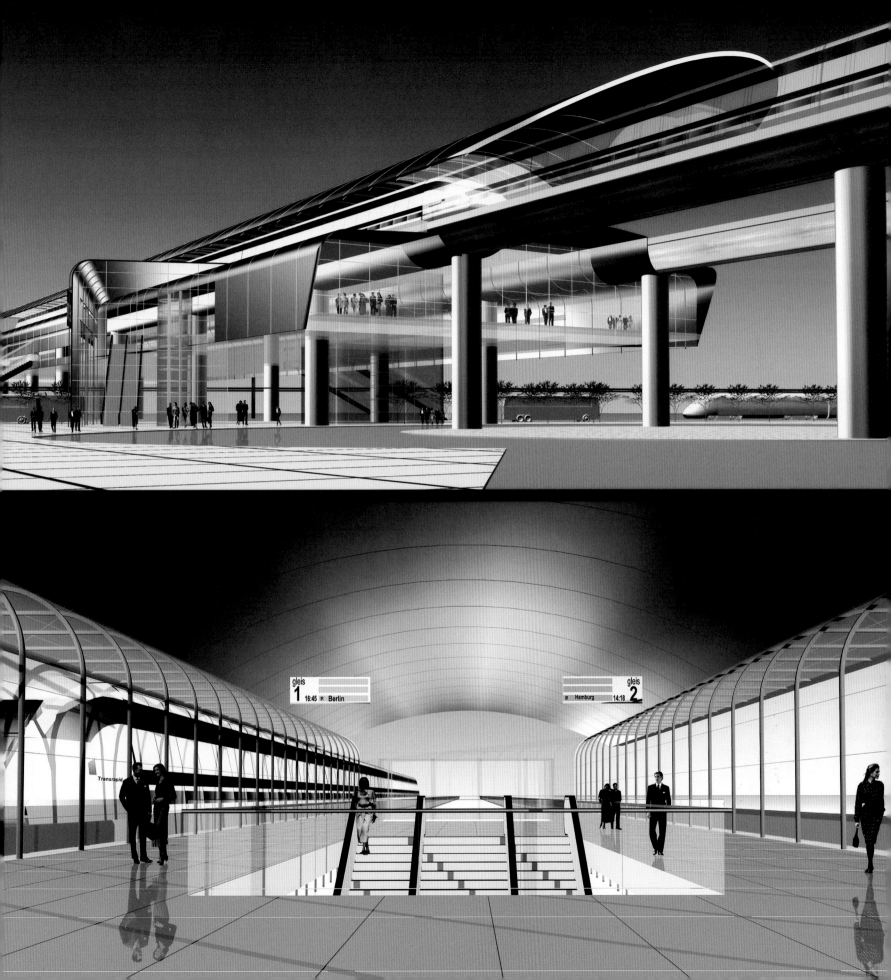

SHANGHAI INTERNATIONAL EXPO CENTRE

China
Design 1998/Completion 2001 (Phase 1)
Client: Shanghai New International Expo
Centre Joint Venture
Shanghai Pudong Land Development
Company; Messe Munich;
Messe Duesseldorf; Hannover Fairs
Helmut Jahn/Werner Sobek/Matthias Schuler
Associate Architect: Shanghai Modern Archi-
tectural Design & Research Institute

The project is a joint venture between a consortium of the fairs of Munich, Düsseldorf and
Hannover with the Pudong Company and was
awarded after an invited competition.

The urban concept of the completed Shanghai
International Expo Centre is like a town. The
halls form a triangle with entries in between,
creating a large town center, which serves as
an open exhibit area. Surrounding this center
are covered arcades, which connect the entries
with all halls. The repeating structures of the
halls form a soft wave, which gives the Shanghai International Expo Centre its unique image.
In the first phase all exhibit halls with an open
exhibit area and one entry hall have been built.
The linear succession of drive, entry hall and the
arcade, tying all halls together, gives a sense of
completeness in this phase and establishes an
image.

Based on our experience on the New Bangkok
International Airport we developed a light
steel-structure with a single layer membrane
stretched over it. This was possible through the
relative short occupancy time during events at
which total comfort has to be achieved. This is
done by decentralized heating and cooling units
located outside the façades in the service-
courts.

The combination of clear-story glazing at the
ends and the side of the high hall give the
spaces natural daylight and a wonderful luminosity at night.

Though technical systems like glazing, metal-
cladding, steel structures and membrane were
based on European or US-standards, it is interesting to note that everything was manufac-
tured in China, except the membrane and the
HVAC-units, which came from Italy and
Malaysia. This serves as a reminder that design
can through innovation challenge conventional
ways of doing things and break new grounds.

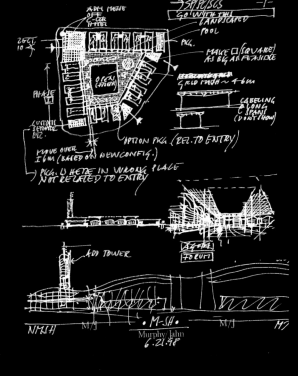

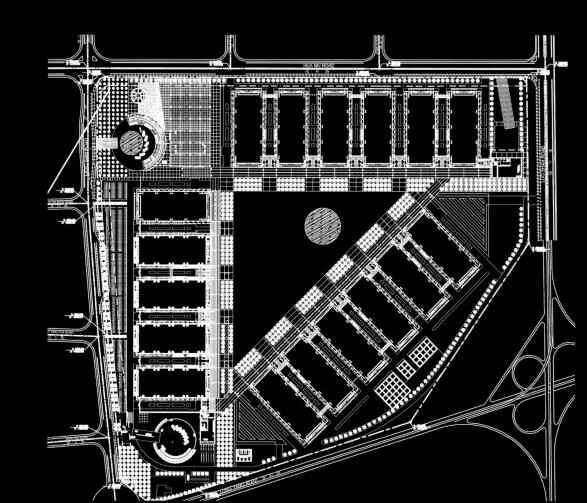

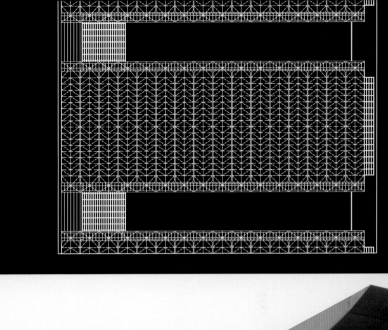

Exhibit hall façade section

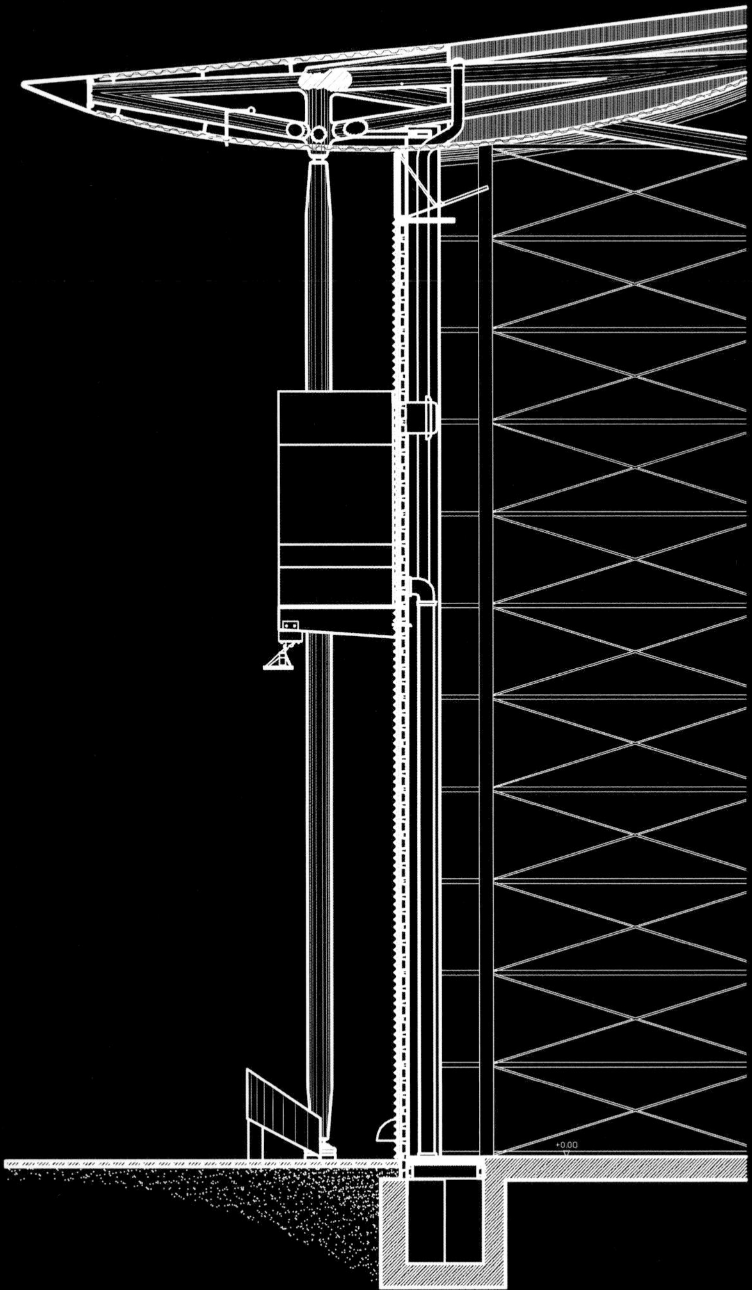

Entry hall façade section

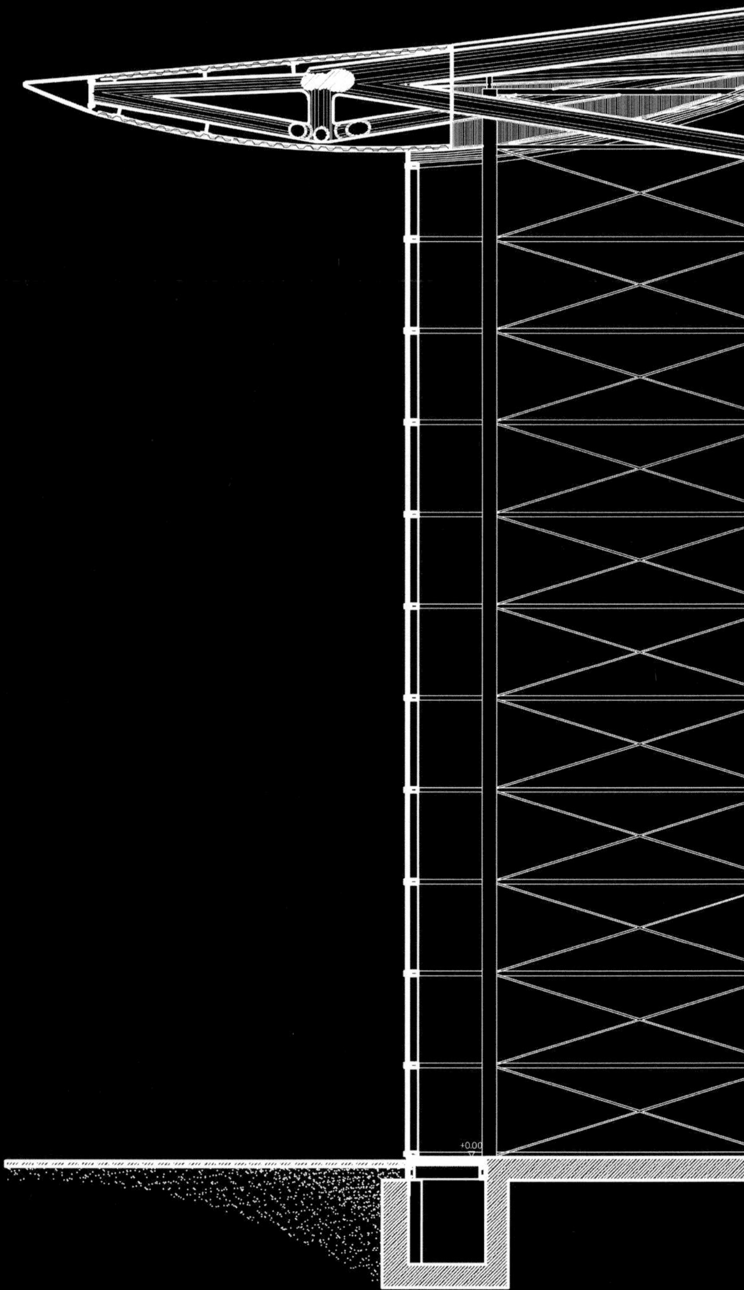

Façade structure

Section thru trusses

SHENZHEN CONVENTION AND
EXHIBIT CENTER

China
Design 1999
Client: Shenzhen Convention & Exhibition Ctr.
Helmut Jahn/Werner Sobek/Matthias Schuler
Associate Architect: China Northeast Building
Design Institute

The commission resulted from an invited international competition.

The curved roof of the Shenzhen Convention and Exhibition Center forms a monumental gate to Shenzhen. Two light membranes of metal and glass overlap to form a rhomboid cover, which wraps over the different functions. At the short ends the roof turns down to the ground. At the long sides the cut reveals the different buildings below the roof and connects through open spaces and the transparency of the buildings the city with Shenzhen Bay.

Due to its location, scale and use, the cellular cladding system developed on the European projects like Bayer and Deutsche Post is simplified and developed as a layered, built-up system. This is the result of our belief in appropriate technology, not necessarily pushing the limits.

To optimize the ventilation efficiency and minimize cooling loads, a flexible displacement ventilation system is proposed, adjustable to the different exhibition layouts. This allows the roof to be kept free of ducts. All other spaces use integrated floor cooling to reduce air supply by 50 %, compared to an all air system.

Political developments forced the project to be cancelled and a new competition was organized for a more central site in the heart of the city.

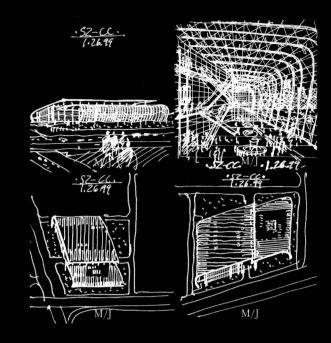

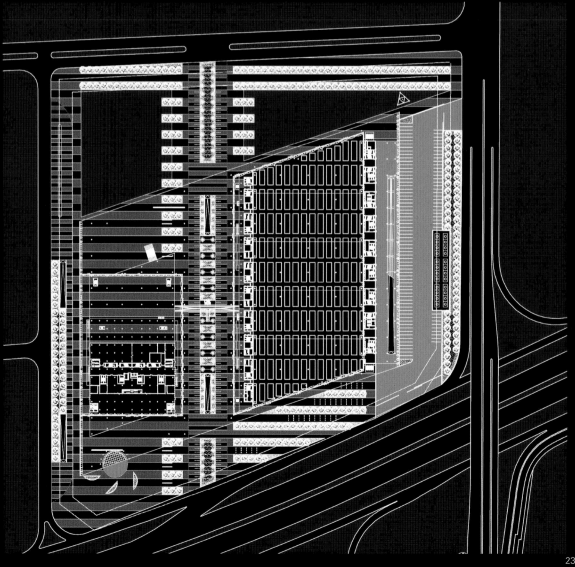

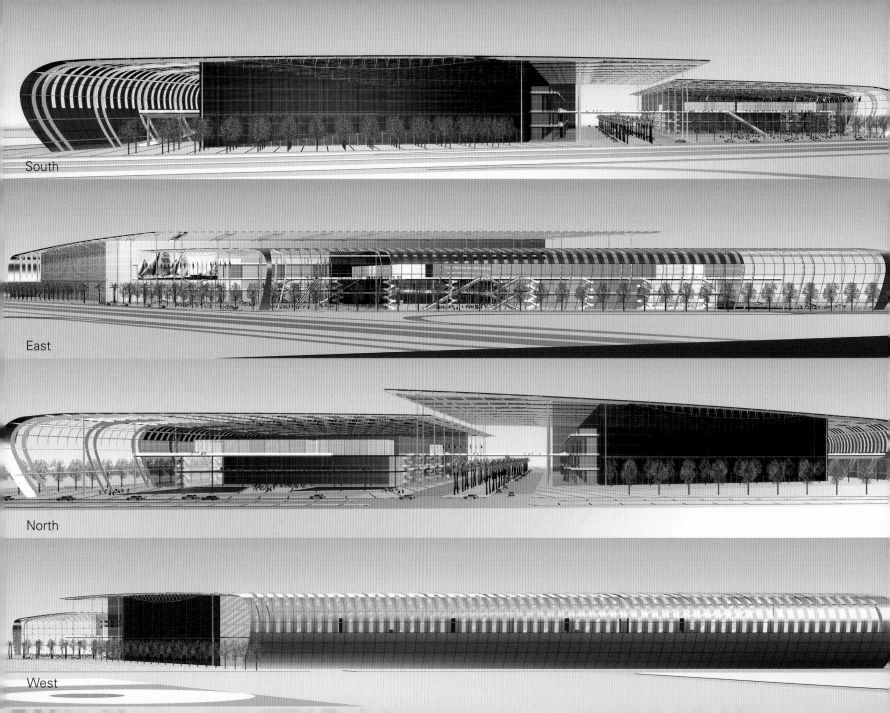

South

East

North

West

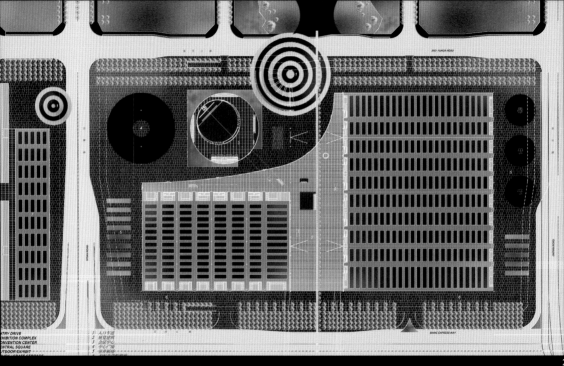

OPERATION STEALTH / DARK STAR

Lake Barrington, Illinois
Design 2000
Client: S.T.R. Industries
Helmut Jahn/Werner Sobek/Matthias Schuler

Stealth, a leading billiard equipment manufacturer and distributor, wanted a building of a progressive image. The project essentially rethinks the building type of the industrial shed for an office/warehouse.

Materials and components developed on previous projects are assembled to suit the program and the US market. A twin-shell membrane is stretched over built-up steel-bends, providing daylight to the office and warehouse spaces and a luminous appearance at night. Heating and cooling is provided through a decentralized system of operable flaps in the façade, backed by power-assisted heating and cooling coils.

The masterplan for the whole site envisions Operation Stealth to be expanded with the Dark Star project, a similar series of industrial containers. The project is presently tied up with zoning and design issues in the conservative community of Lake Barrington.

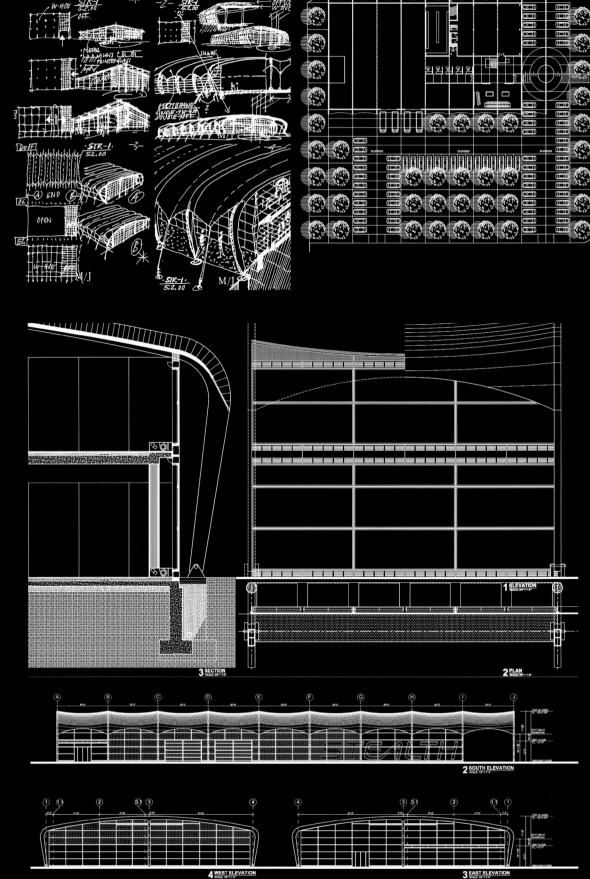

ORIENTAL ART CENTER

Shanghai, China
Design 2001
Client: Shanghai International Tendering Co.
Helmut Jahn/Werner Sobek/Matthias Schuler

Our design entry in an invited competition for the Oriental Arts Center for the Pudong district of Shanghai envisions a light filled, enjoyable building for performance of music and theater.

The organization is very simple and clear. Within the three structural bays the three halls serve different venues and function independently.

The steel structure is of tightly spaced frames. Their ends are glazed, the long façades and the roof are clad in transparent ETFE aircushions with a switchable inner layer, which provides various degrees of sun protection and limits unwanted solar gain. The conditioning is done with low-E systems like integral floor heating and cooling, assisted with displacement air.

The reductions of all the parts lead to a very elegant and sophisticated statement. The entry loggia, the large foyer and the color-coding of the halls elevate this very technical assembly to the appropriate civic quality for the Arts Center.

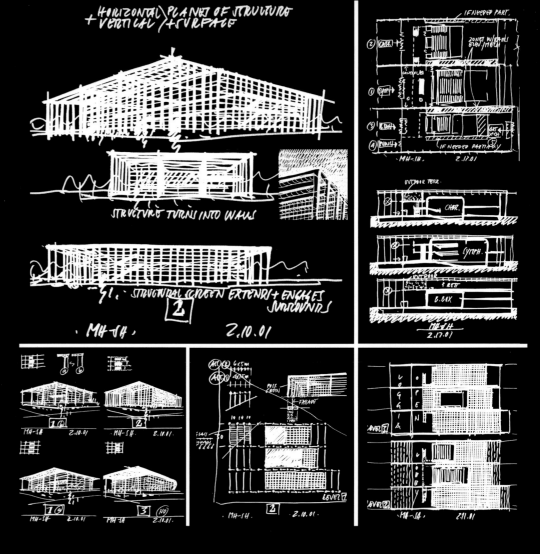

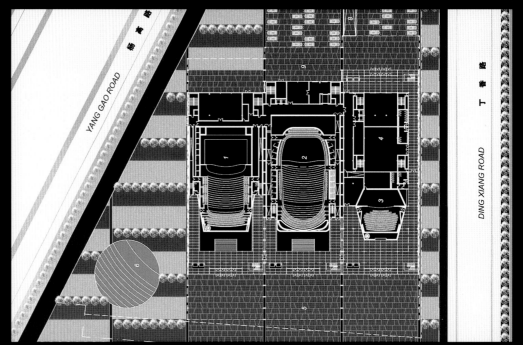

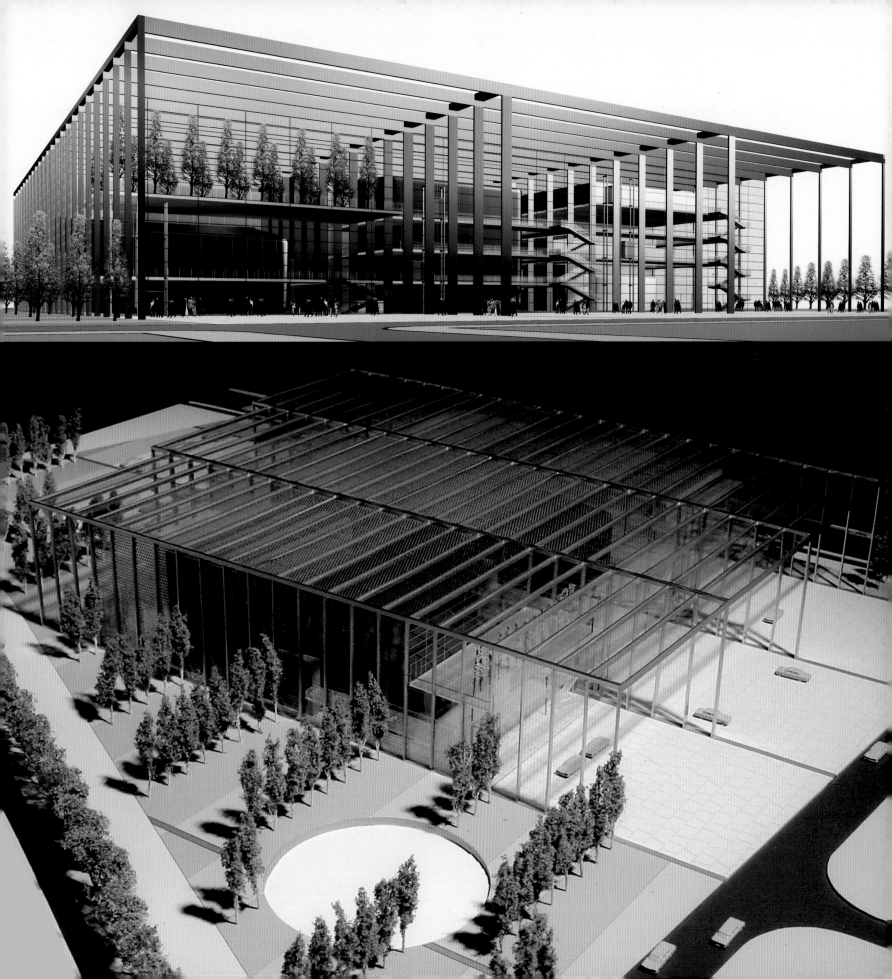

MUNICH STADIUM

Munich, Germany
Design 2001
Client: Bayern/1860 München
Helmut Jahn/Werner Sobek

Our entry for this invited competition for a stadium for the Munich Soccer clubs puts emphasis on the multipurpose aspect of a modern stadium and proposed an advanced technology for an operable roof.

The stadium becomes a new building type, combining the sports center with entertainment and commercial activities. The curved roof not only protects the seating and the field, but creates covered spaces at the north and south ends, which are the points of arrival and departure for the fans.

The building is a clear diagram if its function, construction and materials. All the parts are clearly readable and shape the overall appearance.

The roof creates the unique image along the Autobahn. It is based on the concept of movable segments, like visors, which stack above each other in the open position. The movable and fixed parts above the stands and field are clad with ETFE aircushions. These are UV-resistant and have light transmission of 90 % and guarantee, in a closed position, daylight and the growth of the natural turf. For other events the turf can slide out of the stadium in 3 parts. The remaining roof areas are covered with stainless steel sheets. Thin columns around the perimeter carry the roof loads.

The roof can open or close in 30 minutes and enables different positions. The typical configuration for a soccer game will be either totally open or with covered seats and an open field.

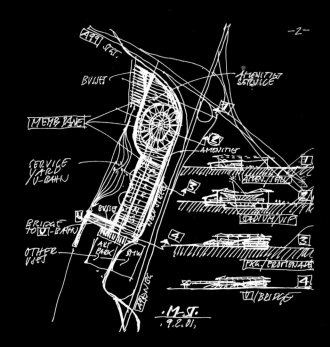

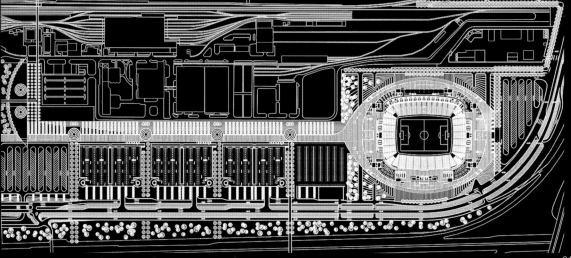

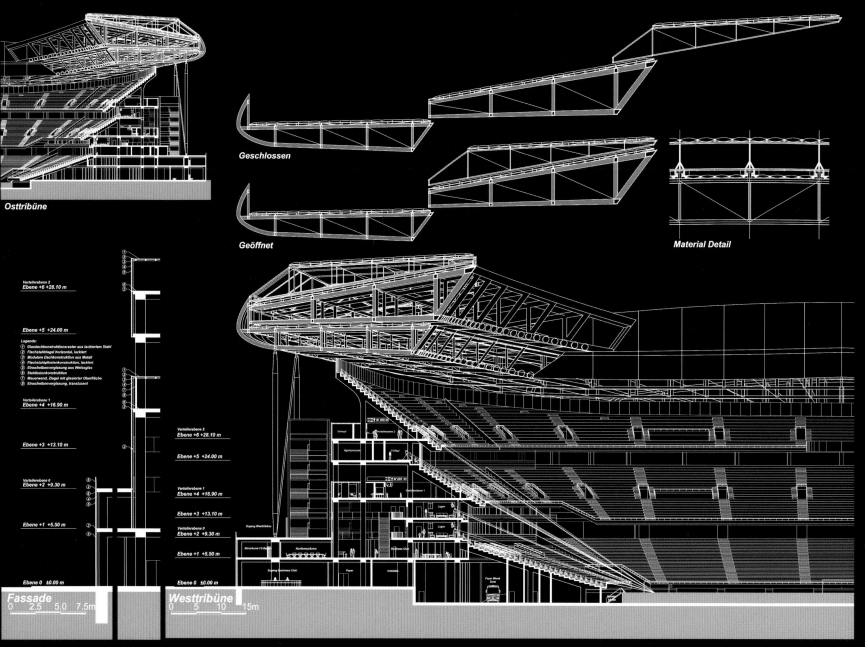

Osttribüne

Geschlossen

Geöffnet

Material Detail

Verteilerebene 2
Ebene +6 +28.10 m

Ebene +5 +24.00 m

Legende:
① Glasdachkonstruktionsraster aus lackiertem Stahl
② Flachstahlriegel horizontal, lackiert
③ Modulare Dachkonstruktion aus Metall
④ Flachstahlpostenkonstruktion, lackiert
⑤ Einscheibenverglasung aus Weissglas
⑥ Stahlbetonkonstruktion
⑦ Mauerwand, Ziegel mit glasierter Oberfläche
⑧ Einscheibenverglasung, transluzent

Verteilerebene 1
Ebene +4 +16.90 m

Ebene +3 +13.10 m

Verteilerebene 0
Ebene +2 +9.30 m

Ebene +1 +5.50 m

Ebene 0 ±0.00 m

Fassade
0   2.5   5.0   7.5m

Verteilerebene 2
Ebene +6 +28.10 m

Ebene +5 +24.00 m

Verteilerebene 1
Ebene +4 +16.90 m

Ebene +3 +13.10 m

Verteilerebene 0
Ebene +2 +9.30 m

Ebene +1 +5.50 m

Ebene 0 ±0.00 m

Westtribüne
0   5   10   15m

Section

TORONTO UNION STATION

Toronto, Canada
Design 2002
Client: Union Pearson Group, Inc.
Helmut Jahn/Werner Sobek

This design was part of the successful proposal of a development team to redevelop the landmarked station and add retail, offices, hotels, apartments and parking. The goal of the proposal is to expand the central business district over the tracks and thereby eliminate the barrier they constitute towards the residential development on the lakefront and to establish a necessary linkage. The project is at once about preserving the symbols of the past and building the symbols of the future.

The conceptual idea is to contrast the historic station with cutting edge modern buildings. The shape of the buildings reminds us of boats moving out on the lake. Their free arrangements maximize the views and make the two tower groups look like tight and complex compositions. The façades are all glass, very transparent and express their uses with subtle difference.

The roof over the tracks is a lightweight steel and glass structure, whose arch rises towards the center of the station.

The towers are positioned to minimize the impact on the existing station, whose 'Great Hall' will be restored and become the focal point of the station and retail activities. At the corners the towers show a purposeful intervention with the landmark. The glass surfaces come down to the ground as screens, producing a layering with the old stone façade, which then becomes like an object displayed in a vitrine – history meets the buildings of today.

The buildings and their systems are 'Archi-Neered' to conserve resources in construction and use. Structure, façade and technical systems are integrated to support each other to achieve utmost simplicity and efficiency.

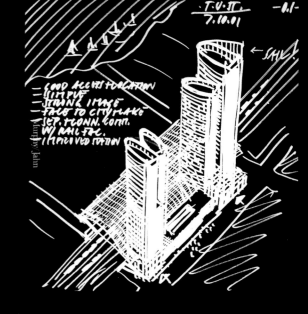

Afterword and Acknowledgements

In this volume, which documents a decade of Helmut Jahn's work, his engineer colleagues Werner Sobek and Matthias Schuler are featured for the first time as equal partners since the high quality of an architectural team can only be assessed through fully integrated solutions.

At the same time, this publication has only been possible through the tireless and co-operative collaboration of all participants, especially the inspired contributions by Helmut Jahn. Keith H. Palmer from the office of Murhpy/Jahn was instrumental in developing the book concept and in compiling the contents as well as assisting with the project descriptions. In deliberate contrast to conventional designs, the architect's colour of choice, black, sets the tone for this publication, enhanced by the exquisite duotone reproductions generated by Photolitho Sturm.

This documentation on "architecture engineering" goes beyond providing an insight into a new evolution in building and the potential for inspiration and new values it contains. It is also an opportunity to appeal to all who are interested in building to expand their horizons: this book could therefore, in a best case scenario, become a handbook of "building identity" for the aesthetically and technologically engaged third generation of architects after Mies, in the spirit of the master's motto: Don't talk, build!

Werner Blaser

MONOGRAPHS

"Helmut Jahn – Design of a New Architecture", Karl Kramer Verlag, 1986

"Helmut Jahn – Extra Edition", A + U Publishing Co., Ltd., 1986

"Helmut Jahn", Nory Miller, Rizzoli International Publications, 1986

"Helmut Jahn Modern Romantic", ed. Ante Glibota, Paris Art Center, 1987

"Helmut Jahn-Airports", Birkhäuser Publishers for Architecture, 1991

"Helmut Jahn, Building Identity", ECON, Executive Verlags GmbH, 1992

"Helmut Jahn 1982–1992", A + U Publishing Co., Ltd., 1992

"Hotel Kempinski", A + U Publishing Co., Ltd., 1995

"Murphy/Jahn, The Master Series", The Images Publishing Company, 1995

"Helmut Jahn-Transparency", 1975–1995, Birkhäuser Publishers for Architecture, 1996

"Archi-Neering, Helmut Jahn/Werner Sobek", Hatje Cantz, 1999

"Murphy Jahn Millennium Series", The Images Publishing Company, 2001

COMPLETED BUILDINGS

1974 KEMPER ARENA, Kansas City, Missouri
1975 AURARIA LIBRARY, Denver, Colorado
1976 FOURTH DISTRICT COURTS BUILDING,
Maywood, Illinois
1976 JOHN MARSHALL COURTS BUILDING,
Richmond, Virginia
1976 H. ROE BARTLE EXHIBITION HALL,
Kansas City, Missouri
1977 MICHIGAN CITY LIBRARY, Michigan City, Indiana
1977 ST. MARY'S ATHLETIC FACILITY,
South Bend, Indiana
1977 MONROE GARAGE, Chicago, Illinois
1977 SPRINGFIELD GARAGE, Springfield, Illinois
1978 GLENBROOK PROFESSIONAL BUILDING,
Northbrook, Illinois
1978 LA LUMIERE GYMNASIUM, La Porte, Indiana
1978 RUST-OLEUM CORPORATE HEADQUARTERS,
Vernon Hills, Illinois
1979 PRAIRIE CAPITAL CONVENTION CENTER –
PARKING GARAGE, Springfield, Illinois
1979 W. W. GRAINGER CORPORATE HEADQUAR-
TERS, Skokie, Illinois
1980 XEROX CENTRE, Chicago, Illinois
1981 DE LA GARZA CAREER CENTER,
East Chicago, Indiana
1981 OAK BROOK POST OFFICE, Oak Brook, Illinois
1981 COMMONWEALTH EDISON DISTRICT
HEADQUARTERS, Bolingbrook, Illinois
1981 AREA 2 POLICE HEADQUARTERS, Chicago, Illinois
1981 ARGONNE PROGRAM SUPPORT FACILITY,
Argonne, Illinois
1982 FIRST SOURCE CENTER, South Bend, Indiana
1982 WISCONSIN RESIDENCE, Eagle River, Wisconsin
1982 ONE SOUTH WACKER OFFICE BUILDING,
Chicago, Illinois
1982 ADDITION TO THE CHICAGO BOARD OF TRADE,
Chicago, Illinois
1983 MERCY HOSPITAL ADDITION, Chicago, Illinois
1983 11 DIAGONAL STREET,
Johannesburg, South Africa
1984 UNIVERSITY OF ILLINOIS AGRICULTURAL ENGIN-
EERING SCIENCE BUILDING, Champaign, Illinois
1984 LEARNING RESOURCES CENTER, COLLEGE OF
DU PAGE, Glen Ellyn, Illinois
1984 PLAZA EAST, Milwaukee, Wisconsin
1984 SHAND MORAHAN CORPORATE HEADQUAR-
TERS, Evanston, Illinois
1984 701 FOURTH AVENUE SOUTH, Minneapolis,
Minnesota
1984 O'HARE RAPID TRANSIT STATION,
Chicago, Illinois
1985 STATE OF ILLINOIS CENTER, Chicago, Illinois
1986 362 WEST STREET, Durban, South Africa
1986 PARKTOWN STANDS 85/879 and 102/103,
Johannesburg, South Africa
1986 METRO WEST, Naperville, Illinois
1986 HAWTHORN CENTER OFFICE BUILDING,
Vernon Hills, Illinois
1986 PARK AVENUE TOWER, New York, New York
1986 300 E. 85th Street, New York, New York
1987 NORTHWESTERN ATRIUM CENTER,
Chicago, Illinois

1987 UNITED AIRLINES TERMINAL,
O'Hare Airport, Chicago, Illinois
1987 ONE LIBERTY PLACE, Philadelphia, Pennsylvania
1987 OAKBROOK TERRACE TOWER,
Oakbrook Terrace, Illinois
1988 MERCHANDISE MART BRIDGE, Chicago, Illinois
1988 WILSHIRE/WESTWOOD OFFICE BUILDING,
Los Angeles, California
1989 425 LEXINGTON AVENUE, New York, New York
1989 750 LEXINGTON AVENUE, New York, New York
1989 CITYSPIRE, New York, New York
1989 MESSEHALLE, Frankfurt, Germany
1990 BARNETT CENTER, Jacksonville, Florida
1991 MESSETURM, Frankfurt, Germany
1991 LIVINGSTON PLAZA, Brooklyn Heights, New York
1991 TWO LIBERTY PLACE, Philadelphia, Pennsylvania
1992 120 N. LaSALLE STREET, Chicago, Illinois
1992 ONE AMERICA PLAZA, San Diego, California
1992 MANNHEIMER LEBENSVERSICHERUNG,
Mannheim, Germany
1992 HYATT REGENCY ROISSY, Roissy, Paris, France
1993 MUNICH ORDER CENTER, Munich, Germany
1993 HITACHI TOWER, Singapore
1993 CALTEX HOUSE, Singapore
1994 HOTEL KEMPINSKI, Munich, Germany
1994 KU'DAMM #70, Berlin, Germany
1994 PALLAS, Stuttgart, Germany
1995 KU'DAMM #119, Berlin, Germany
1996 PRINCIPAL MUTUAL LIFE INSURANCE COM-
PANY, Des Moines, Iowa
1997 RCID ADMINISTRATION BUILDING,
Orlando, Florida
1998 GENERALE BANK NEDERLAND,
Rotterdam, The Netherlands
1998 JC DECAUX BUS SHELTER
1999 EUROPEAN UNION HEADQUARTERS,
Brussels, Belgium
1999 MUNICH AIRPORT CENTER, Munich, Germany
2000 SONY CENTER, Berlin, Germany
2000 AIRPORT KÖLN/BONN, Köln, Germany
2000 SEGERSTROM – IBT, Costa Mesa, California
2000 HA•LO, Chicago, Illinois
2001 NEUES KRANZLER ECK, Berlin, Germany
2002 KAUFHOF GALERIA, Chemnitz, Germany
2002 SHANGHAI INTERNATIONAL EXPO CENTRE,
Shanghai, China
2002 BAYER AG ADMINISTRATION BUILDING,
Leverkusen, Germany

BUILDINGS IN PROGRESS

ILLINOIS INSTITUTE OF TECHNOLOGY STUDENT
HOUSING, Chicago, Illinois
FOCUS MEDIA, Rostock, Germany
BISHOPSGATE, London, England
LANGENSCHEIDT-HOCHHAUS, Munich, Germany
MASTERPLAN NEUTRALE ZONE, AIRPORT MUNICH,
Germany
MANNHEIMER 2, Mannheim, Germany
STEALTH, Barrington, Illinois
MAX, Frankfurt, Germany
O'HARE TERMINALS 1, 2, 3 FACE,
O'Hare International Airport, Chicago, Illinois
DEUTSCHE POST, Bonn, Germany

NEW BANGKOK INTERNATIONAL AIRPORT, Thailand
21 CENTURY TOWER, Shanghai, China
BURBANK MEDIA CENTER, California

AWARDS

KEMPER ARENA SHENZHEN CONVENTION CENTER
1975 AIA National Honor Award
1975 Bartelt Award
1975 AIA Chicago Chapter Award
1975 AISC Award

ABU DHABI CONFERENCE CITY
1976 Progressive Architecture Design Citation
1976 Prize in International Competition

AURARIA LIBRARY
1976 AIA Chicago Chapter Award

XEROX CENTRE
1977 Progressive Architecture Design Citation
1980 AIA Chicago Chapter Award

MICHIGAN CITY LIBRARY
1977 AIA Chicago Chapter Award
1977 AIA Illinois Council Honor Award
1978 AIA American Library Association First Honor
Award
1979 AISC Award

MINNESOTA II
1977 Winner in National Architecture Competition
1978 AIA Chicago Chapter Award
1978 Progressive Architecture Design Citation

ST MARY'S ATHLETIC FACILITY
1977 AIA Chicago Chapter Award
1977 AIA Illinois Council Honor Award
1978 AISC Award
1979 AIA National Honor Award

KANSAS CONVENTION CENTER
1978 AIA Chicago Chapter Award

LA LUMIERE GYMNASIUM
1978 AIA Chicago Chapter Award

OAK BROOK POST OFFICE
1978 AIA Chicago Chapter Award

UNIVERSITY OF ILLINOIS AGRICULTURAL ENGINEERING
SCIENCE BUILDING
1978 AIA Chicago Chapter Award

RUST-OLEUM HEADQUARTERS
1979 AIA Chicago Chapter Award
1979 Young Professional Award by Building Design &
Construction Magazine
1979 AISC Award

ARGONNE PROGRAM SUPPORT FACILITY
1979 Owens-Corning Fiberglas Energy Conservation
Award
1982 AIA Chicago Chapter Award

DE LA GARZA CAREER CENTER
1981   ASHRAE Energy Award
1981   AIA Chicago Chapter Award

COMMONWEALTH EDISON DISTRICT HEADQUARTERS
1981   ASHRAE Energy Award

ADDITION TO THE CHICAGO BOARD OF TRADE
1982   Reliance Development Group, Inc., Second Annual
        Award for Distinguished Architecture
1983   AISC Award
1984   AIA Chicago Chapter Award
1985   Structural Engineering Association of Illinois

ARNOLD W. BRUNNER MEMORIAL PRIZE
IN ARCHITECTURE
1982   Helmut Jahn

AREA 2 POLICE HEADQUARTERS
1983   AIA Chicago Chapter Award

CHICAGO CENTRAL AREA PLAN
1985   Progressive Architecture Award

PLAZA EAST OFFICE CENTER
1985   Distinguished Architect – HELMUT JAHN
        City of Milwaukee Art Commission's 1985 Annual
        Awards

STATE OF ILLINOIS CENTER
1981   ASHRAE Energy Award
1985   Structural Engineering Association of Illinois
1986   AIA Chicago Chapter Award
1991   Ten Best Works of American Architecture
        completed since 1980 AIA
1991   "The Top Ten" Chicago's Ten Most Important Post
        World War II Works of Architecture – Paul Gapp
2001   BOMA – Building of the Year – Chicago Chapter

NORTHWESTERN ATRIUM CENTER
1986   Structural Engineering Association of Illinois
2001   BOMA – Building of the Year – Chicago Chapter

701 FOURTH AVENUE SOUTH
1986   AIA New York State Award

O'HARE RAPID TRANSIT STATION
1987   AIA National Honor Award
1988   NEA Presidential Design Award

METRO WEST
1987   AIA Chicago Chapter Award

UNITED AIRLINES TERMINAL
1987   Structural Engineering Association of Illinois
1987   AIA National Honor Award
1988   R.S. Reynolds Memorial Award
1988   Annual Design Review -
        "Best of Category", Industrial Design Magazine
1988   AIA Chicago Chapter Award
1989   American Consulting
1990   AIA Chicago Chapter Divine Detail Honor Award
1990   Quaternario, International Award for Innovative
        Technology in Architecture

1990   AISC Award
1991   Ten Best Works of American Architecture complet-
        ed since 1980
1999   The Best Interior Design of the Late 20th Century

O'HARE INTERNATIONAL AIRPORT
1988   AIA Chicago Chapter Twenty-Five Year Award

CITYSPIRE
1987   Annual Award – Concrete Industry Board of
        New York

R.S. REYNOLDS MEMORIAL AWARD
1988   Annual Award for Distinguished Architecture Using
        Aluminum United Airlines Terminal

CHEVALIER dans L'ORDRE des ARTS et des LETTRES
1988   Helmut Jahn, Ministere de la Culture et de la
        Communication, Paris, France

DOMINO'S 30 AWARD
1989
1990

ONE LIBERTY PLACE
1990   AIA Chicago Chapter Award
1990   AISC Award

MESSEHALLE
1991   AIA Chicago Chapter Award

WILSHIRE/WESTWOOD
1991   AIA Chicago Chapter Award
1991   "TOP 100 ARCHITECTS" – ARCHITECTURAL
        DIGEST
1991   TEN MOST INFLUENTIAL LIVING AMERICAN
        ARCHITECTS – AMERICAN INSTITUTE OF ARCHI-
        TECTS
1991   DEAN OF ARCHITECTURE AWARD – CHICAGO
        DESIGN AWARDS 120 NORTH LASALLE
1991   DEVELOPMENT OF THE YEAR – CHICAGO SUN
        TIMES REAL ESTATE
1992   AIA Chicago Chapter Award
1993   New Chicago Architecture
1995   Structural Engineering Association of Illinois
2001   BOMA – Building of the Year – Chicago Chapter

1992   IIT AWARD FOR OUTSTANDING CONTRIBUTION
        TO THE BUILT ENVIRONMENT

1992   CHICAGO ARCHITECTURE AWARD
        THE AMERICAN INSTITUTE OF ARCHITECTS/
        ILLINOIS AND THE MERCHANDISE MART

ONE AMERICA PLAZA – TROLLEY STATION
1992   AIA San Diego Chapter Award

MANNHEIMER LEBENSVERSICHERUNG
1992   AIA Chicago Chapter Award
1993   Bund Deutscher Architekten

ILLINOIS ACADEMY OF FINE ARTS
1993   OUTSTANDING ACHIEVEMENT/ARCHITECT

HITACHI TOWER
1993 CIDB Best Buildable Design Awards

CALTEX HOUSE
1994 CIDB Best Buildable Design Awards

MUNICH ORDER CENTER
1994   AIA Chicago Chapter Award
1996   AIA National Honor Award

HYATT REGENCY ROISSY
1994   AIA Chicago Chapter Award (Interior Architecture)

HOTEL KEMPINSKI
1995   AIA Chicago Chapter Award
1995   AIA Chicago Chapter Divine Detail Award
1998   American Society of Landscape Architects
1998   Bundesverband Garten-, Landschafts- und
        Sportplatzbau "International Trend Prize – Building
        with Green"

KU'DAMM #70
1995   AIA Chicago Chapter Award
1996   AIA National Honor Award

BUS SHELTER
1998   The DuPont Benedictus Award

MUNICH AIRPORT CENTER
1999   International Prize for Textile Architecture 1999
2002   AIA Chicago Chapter Award

SONY CENTER
1993   New Chicago Architecture
2001   Urban Land Institute
2001   AIA Chicago Chapter Award
2002   Deutscher Stahlbau Award

DEUTSCHE POST
2001   Urban Land Institute

HA•LO
2001   AIA Chicago Chapter Award
2001   Chicago Building Congress Award
2001   National Design Building Award

IMPERIAL BANK TOWER RENOVATION
2002   Innovation Design and Excellence in Architecture
        using Structural Steel

NEUES KRANZLER ECK
2002   AIA Chicago Chapter Award

FLUGHAFEN KÖLN/BONN
2002   Deutscher Stahlbau Award

EXHIBITIONS

1974/86 Exhibitions, AIA Chicago Chapter Awards, The Art Institute of Chicago

1977 October – Participant in symposium "State of the Art of Architecture/77", Graham Foundation, Chicago Illinois

1977 Member, "Chicago 7"

1977 December – Participant in group show "Exquisite Corpse", Walter Kelly Gallery, Chicago Illinois

1978 December – Participant in group show "Townhouses", Walker Art Center, Minneapolis Minnesota

1979 Participant 25th Annual Progressive Architecture Awards Jury, New York, New York

1980 April – Exhibition "City Segments", Walker Art Center, Minneapolis, Minnesota

1980 May – Exhibition "Late Entries to the Chicago Tribune Competition", Museum of Contemporary Art, Chicago, Illinois

1980 June – Exhibition "The Presence of the Past", representing USA Biennale, Venice, Italy; 1981-82 Paris, France; San Francisco, California

1980 August – Exhibition "The Architectural Process", Young-Hoffman Gallery, Chicago, Illinois

1980 October – Participant in symposium "Designing Today for Tomorrow", Architectural League of New York, New York

1981 The Fort Worth Art Museum, Fort Worth, Texas

1981 January – Exhibition "Chicago Architectural Drawing", Frumkin & Struve, Chicago, Illinois

1981 March – Exhibition – The Chicago Architectural Club, Graham Foundation, Chicago, Illinois

1981 May – Chicago International Art Exhibit, Navy Pier, Chicago, Illinois

1981 December – Exhibition "Architecture as Synthesis", Harvard University Graduate school of Design, Cambridge, Massachusetts

1981/82 May – Arnold W. Brunner Memorial Prize, and exhibit, American Academy and Institute of Arts and Letters, New York, New York

1982 August – Exhibition – The Chicago Architectural Club, The Art Institute of Chicago, Chicago, Illinois

1982 October – Exhibition "Chicago Architects Design", The Art Institute of Chicago, Chicago, Illinois

1982 November – Exhibition – Yale University, School of Architecture, New Haven, Connecticut

1982 November – Exhibition "Contemporary Chicago Architecture", Festival of the Arts, Northern Illinois University, DeKalb, Illinois

1983 February – Exhibition "The Architect's Vision From Sketch to Final Drawing", The Chicago Historical Society, Chicago, Illinois

1983 February – Exhibition "Current Projects", Thomas Beeby, Lawrence Booth, Helmut Jahn, Krueck and Olson, Stanley Tigerman, Young-Hoffman Gallery Chicago, Illinois

1983 March – Exhibition "Ornamentalism: The New Decorativeness in Architecture and Design", The Hudson River Museum, New York, New York, Archer M. Huntington Art Gallery, University of Texas, Austin, Texas

1983 May – Exhibition "New Chicago Architecture 1983", The Art Institute of Chicago, Chicago, Illinois

1983 May – Participant in symposium "Minneapolis Profile 1983", Walker Art Center, Minneapolis, Minnesota

1983 June – Exhibition "Tall Buildings", The Southern Chapter Alberta Association of Architects, Calgary, Alberta, Canada

1983 September – Exhibition "Design USA", Castello Sforzasco in the Sala Viscontea, Milano, Italy

1983 October – Exhibition "Surface and Ornament", Puck Building, New York, New York

1983 October – Exhibition "Competitions Won and Lost", San Francisco AIA Headquarters Gallery, San Francisco, California

1983 October – Exhibition "150 Years of Chicago Architecture", Paris Art Center, Paris, France

1983 November – Exhibition "1992 Chicago World's Fair Design Conference Drawings, New York, Los Angeles, Chicago", The University of Illinois, Chicago Campus, Chicago, Illinois

1983 November – Exhibition "100 Years of Architectural Drawings in Chicago", Illinois Bell Telephone Company, Chicago, Illinois

1983 November – Exhibition – The Chicago Architectural Club, "Tops" and Members' Work, The Art Institute of Chicago, Chicago, Illinois

1984 February – Exhibition "Helmut Jahn", Ballenford Architectural Books and Gallery, Ltd., Toronto, Ontario, Canada

1984 March – Exhibition "Chicago and New York, More than a Century of Architectural Interaction", The Art Institute of Chicago; The A.I.A. Foundation, The Octagon, Washington, D.C.; Farish Gallery, Rice University, Houston, Texas; The New York Historical Society, New York, New York

1984 June – Opening, permanent architectural collection Deutsches Architekturmuseum, Frankfurt am Main, Germany

1984 November – Exhibition "Art and Architecture/ Design", Moosart Gallery, Miami, Florida

1984 November – Exhibition – The Chicago Architectural Club, Members' Work, The Art Institute of Chicago, Chicago, Illinois

1984 December – Exhibition "The State of Illinois Center", University of Illinois, Champaign-Urbana, Illinois

1985 January – Exhibition "Exhibition on Advanced Structures", Syracuse University, Syracuse, New York

1985 March – Exhibition "Vu de l'Interieur ou la Raison de l'Architecture" – "Looking from the Inside or the Reason of Architecture", Paris Biennale, Paris, France

1985 September/December "Contemporary Landscape – from the Horizon of Postmodern Design", The National Museums of Modern Art, Kyoto and Tokyo, Japan

1985 October – Exhibition "150 Years of Chicago Architecture", Museum of Science and Industry, Chicago, Illinois

1986 January – Exhibition – The Chicago Architectural Club – Members' Work, Betsy Rosenfield Gallery, Chicago, Illinois

1986 February – Exhibition "Modernism Redux: Critical Alternatives", Grey Art Gallery and Study Center, New York University, New York, New York

1986 June – Exhibition "Vision der Moderne", Deutsches Architekturmuseum, Frankfurt, Germany, October: The National Museum of Modern Art, Tokyo

1986 October – Exhibition "Helmut Jahn", Gallery MA, Tokyo, Japan

1986 October – Exhibition "New Chicago Skyscrapers", Gallery of Design of the Merchandise Mart, Chicago, Illinois

1987 January – Exhibition "What Could Have Been: Unbuilt Architecture of the 80's", Dallas Market Center, Dallas, TX.

1987 May – Exhibition "GA International '87", GA Gallery, Tokyo, Japan

1987 June - Exhibition "Helmut Jahn", Architekturgalerie, Munich, Germany

1987 July – Exhibition "New Chicago Skyscrapers", Merchandise Mart, Chicago, Illinois

1987 September – Exhibition "Helmut Jahn", Paris Art Center, Paris, France

1987 December – Exhibition "What Could Have Been: Unbuilt Architecture of the 80's", Chicago Architecture Foundation, Chicago, Illinois

1988 May – Exhibition "The Experimental Tradition", The Architectural League, New York, New York

1988 July – Exhibition "New Chicago Skyscrapers", ArchiCenter Gallery, Chicago, Illinois

1988 August – Exhibition "Experimental Skytowers", Rizzoli International Bookstore, Chicago, Illinois

1988 September – Exhibition "The Cities of the World and the Future of the Metropolis," Triennale di Milano, Italy

1988 October – Exhibition "The Art of Design", University of Milwaukee Fine Arts Galleries, Milwaukee, Wisconsin

1988 November – Exhibition "The Postmodern Explained to Children", Bonne Fanten Museum, Maastricht, The Netherlands

1989 January - Exhibition "The Art of Design," "One Liberty Place," "Bank of the Southwest Tower," STA Gallery, Chicago, Illinois

1989 March – Exhibition "Architecture in New York," "Columbus Circle," "Times Square," "Terminalgebäude für AA and North Western," JFK Deutsches Architekturmuseum, Germany

1989 June – Exhibition "Original Unpublished Drawings and Models by Chicago Architectural Club Members," Ruth Volid Gallery, Ltd., Chicago, Illinois

1989 September – Exhibition "Design USA – A.U.S. – U.S.S.R. Cultural Exchange Exhibition", United States Information Agency, U.S.S.R.

1989 September – Exhibition "Competitions in Architecture," The Architectural League of New York, New York, New York

1989 October – Exhibition "Tall Buildings," Brisbane, Australia

1989 October – Exhibition "Tall Buildings," West Perth, Australia

1989	November – Exhibition "New Chicago Architecture," Metropolitan Press, Chicago, Illinois
1990	Exhibition "Chicago Architecture," Lisbon, Portugal, Gulbenkian Foundation
1990	May – Exhibition "The Socially Responsible Environment: US/USSR 1980–1990," Architects Designers Planners for Social Responsibility, USA, and USSR Union of Architects, New York, New York
1990	June – Exhibition "Celebrate Chicago Architecture", Metropolitan Press, Union Station in Washington, D.C.
1990	September – Exhibition "Terminus to Interchange", The Building Centre Trust, London
1991	January – Exhibition "New Chicago Architecture", The Chicago Athenaeum, Illinois
1991	November – Exhibition "Helmut Jahn" YKK – Cupples Design Forum Tokyo, Japan
1992	January – Exhibition "Celebrating 75 Years of Chicago Architecture", The Arts Club of Chicago, Illinois
1992	November through 1993 December – From Mars to Main Street: America Designs
1993	March – American Skyscrapers, Helsinki, Finland
1993	March – "New Chicago Architecture Exhibition" (Fort Canning Tower, Hyatt), Europa-Haus, Chicago, Illinois
1993	May – Chicago Architecture and Design: 1923–1993, Art Institute
1993	June – The Art of Design, Milwaukee, Wisconsin
1993	September – City-Projects, Berlin Pavilion, Berlin, Germany
1993	September – Buenos Aires Biennial of Architecture '93, Recent Work at the Museum of Fine Arts
1994	January – ARCAM Galerie (Hyatt), Amsterdam, The Netherlands

1994	November – Exhibition "New Chicago Architecture", The Chicago Athenaeum
1995	"Helmut Jahn Towards Romantic Modernism, 1985–1995 Gallery MA", Exhibition 1995, Tokyo, Japan
1996	March – The Art of Design, Northern Illinois University
1996	"Helmut Jahn/Transparency", "The Prairie Avenue Bookshop", Chicago, Illinois
1997	"An Exhibition of Airport Designs" (United Airlines Terminal One Complex), The Architectural Association, School of Architecture, London, United Kingdom
1997	"Costantini Museum Competition" A Honoree Mention, Brazil
1998	"Unbuilt Cincinnati Exhibition" (Fountain Square West), The Cincinnati Forum, Ohio
1999	"Archi-Neering", Städtisches Museum Leverkusen Schloß Morsbroich, Leverkusen, Germany
1999	"Helmut Jahn Drawings", The Renaissance Society at the University of Chicago, Illinois
1999	"Material Evidence" (Bus Shelter), Museum of Contemporary Art, Chicago, Illinois "Skyscrapers: The New Millennium"
2000	August – Exhibition The Art Institute of Chicago, Illinois
2001	"Blue Stage", Haus der Kulturen der Welt GmbH, Berlin, Germany
2000	"Skyscrapers: The New Millennium", August, The Art Institute of Chicago, Illinois
2002	"Helmut Jahn, Archi-Neering", January, Mandeville Gallery, Union College, New York
2002	"World Airports – Weltflughäfen", Deutsches Museum, Frankfurt, Germany

Rendering Credits

Scott Becker: pp. 140, 141

Francisco Gonzalez-Pulido: pp. 133, 192, 196, 197, 199, 202, 203, 205, 206, 207, 209, 211

Yorgo Lykourgiotis: pp. 129, 130, 131, 143, 144, 145

T.J. McLeish: pp. 157, 213, 216, 217, 224, 225, 239, 241, 243, 247

John Manaves: pp. 123, 125, 126, 127, 159, 183, 189

Robert Muller: pp. 135, 137, 146, 147, 149, 151, 153, 154, 187, 191, 253, 254, 255

Alphonso Peluso: pp. 108, 109, 113, 169, 171, 179

Vertex Graphics, Inc.: pp. 227, 228, 229, 231, 245, 249, 251